INSIDE CABIN
WITH BALCONY

MARCO STRÖHLEIN was the host of various light entertainment programmes on German television from 1996 to 2003. In recent years he has gained a reputation as a presentation skills trainer. His job entailed numerous engagements on cruise ships, where he introduced the crew members to the art of compering and drew on his personal experience to create a comedy act. Here he also profited from his tenacious scepticism towards everyone he's not closely related to. He tours with his stand-up comedy throughout Europe and on cruise ships all over the world.

MICHAEL TASCHE is a freelance author, coach and film director. For many years he specialised in TV comedies and wrote for top German comedians as well as scripting sitcoms. He also devised and staged shows for German celebrities. For the past 12 years Michael Tasche has worked for various cruise operators as a writer, coach and inspirational advisor. His natural inquisitiveness, innate powers of observation and a talent for exaggeration laid the foundation for the stories in this book.

Marco Ströhlein

Michael Tasche

# INSIDE CABIN
# WITH
# BALCONY

## THE ULTIMATE A–Z CRUISE GUIDE

9th German Edition November 2016 /
1st English Edition December 2018
© 2012 Marco Ströhlein / Michael Tasche
Translation by: Martina Lammers &
Andrea Dutton-Kölbl
Cover Design, Illustrations and Layout: Max Baitinger
(www.max-baitinger.com)
Printed by: Tolek
Distributed by: MS Entertainment UG
All rights reserved
ISBN 978-3-9819151-0-5
www.cruise-fanshop.com

## DEDICATED TO:

Odo de Châtillon (a.k.a. Urban II, 1035–1099, Pope), who initiated the first pleasure cruise through the eastern Mediterranean for bored knights and noblemen, thus sowing the seeds for the concept of a "cruisade" in 1095 – an idea which wouldn't be reinstated for another 800 years.

## MANY THANKS TO:

Mladec the Fifth (32,854–32,812 B.C., non-swimmer, hunter and gatherer), who hit on the idea of crossing a river perched on a tree trunk.

and

Johannes Gutenberg (1400–1468, entrepreneur), who conceived the idea of the printing press.

Without those two this book may have never seen the light of day in its present format.

# INDEX

## HIGHLIGHTS

# PREFACE

As the popular song goes "Oh, I do like to be beside the seaside", but even more so on the actual sea. The fun of it all! Yet fun is by no means the only alluring aspect of a cruise as it is undoubtedly the most comfortable and luxurious way of acquainting oneself with as many cities and regions as possible in just a matter of days – provided they are close to a port, that is. A cruise is basically like carrying one's own hotel from one place to the next, including full board and one's fellow lodgers. Because one meets a lot of people on a cruise. Wildly different people. People one may also encounter at the supermarket, at the opera or a soccer match – some of them consecutively on all three occasions. And this doesn't just apply to the passengers but also to the crew.

Mark Twain once said: "I wonder if God created man because He was disappointed with the monkey" and surmised that God didn't bother experimenting any further after that. Which is kind of a shame as the end result could, no doubt, have been improved upon.

What some (few) people get up to on their voyage is quite entertaining. Some of their escapades are born out of ignorance, some out of vanity and others out of stupidity. This guide endeavours to remedy the first two causes. As far as the third is concerned, no promises can be made. Be that as it may, a cruise is the best things since sliced bread. Despite or actually because of the people who embark on it. This book will teach you a lot about both.

## ANCHORS AWEIGH

The ship's departure is the moment that indelibly burns itself into the passenger's emotional memory, never to be erased again. The moment one has eagerly anticipated for months, imagined over and over again based on reminiscences of The Love Boat, has finally arrived.

The Captain introduces that exceedingly uplifting point in time with the helpful and informative announcement: "Welcome aboard, ladies and gentlemen. We're about to cast off and will soon be on the way to our first port of call." And then the cruise actually starts. Now all your worries literally fall away from you, just like the heavy hawsers being released from the bollards plunge into the sea. The lines are pulled on board while the propellers churn up white foam, the special departure tune blasts from the loudspeakers, the ship starts moving, the typhon (also see Typhon), the ship's horn in layman's terms, sounds three times and the harbour master replies. The crowd waving from the pier doesn't know any of the passengers who also don't know any of those people, wave back at them, and everyone's happy. But the honking harbour master and waving strangers presumably serve just one purpose: to distract from the sight that's gradually being revealed beneath the foam surrounding the propellers in the dock. Because now everything that has been dumped there for generations is being tossed about and forced to the surface: bicycles, mummified cats, plastic bags with exotic labels, wellingtons, bits of fish, car tyres and, depending on the location, the occasional long-lost brother-in-law, wrapped up in a carpet.

But you won't notice any of this on your first cruise. You will be totally enchanted and relish the experience. Not even reading this book will change that.

# ARRIVAL

Rumour has it that the holiday begins as soon as you embark on your outward journey. Not necessarily so. The day starts at four in the morning when your brother-in-law, the designated driver to the airport, has overslept. There are only two middle seats left on the plane, 15 rows apart. Scared of flying, SHE inadvertently scratches the hand of the stranger beside her during take-off, which is the moment HE realises that his heart medication is in the suitcase instead of his hand luggage. Speaking of luggage – although your suitcase has been taken straight to the cabin (also see Cabin), its allegedly indestructible hard shell hasn't quite survived the 75 foot drop from the plane to the ground. One frequently has to relinquish it as much as the hope of reclaiming it undamaged.

At this stage most travellers will also have relinquished the illusion of a comfortable arrival. And our wary voyagers are still a long way from (hopefully) being reunited with their luggage in their cabin. Especially when taking a cruise to far distant regions such as South America or Asia one can observe people climbing up the gangway (also see Gangway) who look like they've covered the entire 6000 miles on foot. With their suitcase. When those poor, tortured package tourists finally manage the last few steps of that very gangway at 45 degrees in the shade and are greeted by the well-intended "Did you have a pleasant journey?" it is presumably sheer willpower and/or the lack of physical strength which prevents them from resorting to violence.

But the travellers' condition after their arrival is not only determined by the length of the outward journey or the local temperature, it is also greatly influenced by the choice of transport, i.e. the airline. Sadly it is not allowed to mention names for legal reasons. Suffice it to say that the three airlines whose services considerably contribute towards their clientele's need of a holiday are respectively based in Spain, the Netherlands and Ireland. If you have involuntarily massaged the lower back region of the person in front of you with your kneecaps for twelve hours and your new seat is on the toilet after partaking of the in-flight menu, you are a guest of one of these companies. Their devoted stewardesses are also far past their first bloom. As the flight attendants' average age is at least twice that of the fleet's oldest plane, one sometimes refers to them as the hearing aid brigade. A reasonably young man is easily tempted to offer his seat to these ladies and will occasionally wonder who will save whom in an emergency.

After a stressful outward journey the thrill of anticipation towards the cruise is vastly increased; the guest is satisfied with the least bit of luxury and instantly feels on top of the world on "his" cruise ship. This does, naturally, raise the suspicion that the cruise company and the airline have perhaps secretly ... come to an... but that would be going too far.

# ATLANTIC CROSSING

One of the last great adventures which may still be enjoyed as a package tourist must surely be an Atlantic crossing. At least in the opinion of many an expectant cruise enthusiast who has booked just that with at least five successive days at sea; in other words five days without one's feet touching solid ground.

The Atlantic! The route taken by Leif Erikson and Magellan, the home of giant octopuses und killer sharks, of storms and hurricanes with gigantic waves and wild whitecaps. Something one has to have experienced, no, conquered. With a bit of luck all these may be seen on the northern route across the Big Pond. But in most cases a journey like this is completely uneventful and peaceful, particularly when choosing the well-loved southern route towards the Caribbean. The sun smiles from a cloudless sky each morning and the sea is as calm as a Tibetan lama. The only dangerous aspect, the destructive and unpredictable element, is the mood among the passengers who are bored out of their wits. Should an attentive crew be unsuccessful in channelling the emotions which are about to erupt, they'll suddenly all make an appearance: the giant octopuses and killer sharks, the storms and hurricanes and, naturally, also the gigantic waves and wild whitecaps – and all those personified in one or the other of the guests. The cruisader who survives the experience will feel like having been knighted. This certainly applies to the passengers and even more so to the crew.

## BOOZE

On board alcohol is readily available in the same vast quantities as food. The larger ocean liners boast at least ten bars and as such the ratio to their clientele is very much in favour of the latter with roughly one bar to every 210 passengers. A ratio which makes Magaluf and Torremolinos look like gastronomically underdeveloped nature reserves. There are plenty of occasions aboard for a little nightcap or a major piss up, solely based on strict maritime traditions, of course, and not at all related to a heightened need for strong liquor. Old seafaring rituals include (amongst others) raising glasses on crossing the Suez, Panama and White Sea-Baltic canals as well as the Straits of Gibraltar and the Dardanelles (also see Dardanelles). It goes without saying that a hearty swig is also called for before and after circumnavigating the infamous Cape Horn. In addition there's the glass of bubbly when putting out to sea, the drop of whiskey from gale force 7 onwards and the five beers on the first day on the ocean. Sooner or later most passengers tire of fabricating sanctimonious excuses and no longer even blush when ordering their tenth gin and tonic at the pool bar. It would be quite impossible to get any more red in the face, anyhow, as everyone around the pool will have already achieved their maximum redness level. Those adversely affected by overindulgence in alcoholic beverages can always disguise their sad state as seasickness. But here the men in particular find themselves in a predicament. Both conditions are rather embarrassing from the perspective of social acceptability and mark the sufferer as a wimp or pansy. In this case the only remedy is to urge the rest of one's party to drink just as much so one's own condition isn't quite as obvious.

The real test, however, is faced by the individuals who laid their glorious past with Messrs Jim Beam and Johnny Walker and the Hops and Malt family to rest years ago. Three days into the journey at the latest they'll be fed up having to explain themselves and sneakily have their mineral water served in a champagne bottle. The big plus: four bottles later they'll have earned the undivided admiration of those who regard the voyage mainly as endurance training for their liver.

# BINGO

The oldest game aboard a cruise liner is shuffleboard (also see Shuffleboard); the second oldest is bingo. Anyone able to read the numbers between 1 and 99, who doesn't need to use his fingers when counting and who can mark a square on his card with a cross, can play it. Bingo is basically easier than playing lotto because the decision of which numbers to pick is made for you. Also unlike lotto the aim of the game is to place a cross on all the numbers on your card. Seeing that the players have far less than 59 numbers on their sheets, it doesn't take quite as long as most people fear. The limited number of numbers on the cards not only ensures shorter games but also a winner of the cash paid in by everyone beforehand on the night. Once a player has managed to completely fill his card with crosses, he has to announce this by shouting "Bingo!". Hence the name. The game is great fun and suitable for all ages.

As bingo is the only on-board entertainment which doesn't require too much physical exertion, it was introduced quite early on American liners, the first modern cruise ships, where the players were primarily elderly ladies while the gentlemen divvied up the world between them in the smokers' lounge. These elderly ladies often exhibited the same slightly deformed and even more slightly wobbly underside of their upper arms (caused by their delight in the extensive on-board menu and the loss of connective tissue firmness), particularly visible when raising their arms while exclaiming "Bingo!" This quickly led to contemptuous American fitness instructors labelling the feature as "bingo wings".

A quick and spirited exclamation of "Bingo!" once your card is filled is the key to happiness as it is quite possible that several players are able to tick all their numbers during the same round. In that case the fastest caller wins according to the old Darwinian law, also known as the survival of the fittest. Once the common bingo player is therefore down to his last unticked square, his adrenaline level rises enormously. The body immediately prepares to jump, rather like Neanderthals getting ready to run hell for leather at the unexpected and unwelcome arrival of a sabre-toothed tiger. Should one of the players happen to have the last number to complete the card, a slow motion study would beautifully illustrate the peak performance the human body is capable of: identifying the last number called as correct, placing a cross in the vacant square while lifting one's arm and simultaneously yelling "Bingo!" takes all of 0.2 seconds.

The excessive adrenaline release, if unused, that means whenever someone else once again finished before you, inevitably damages the coronary vessels and as such motivated the game masters on many a ship to connect certain numbers with certain actions. On the one hand this burns dangerous excess adrenaline, on the other it immeasurably increases the impact value of the game; a fact also much appreciated by the players. It was only at the very last minute that the most creative game hosts could be stopped in their tracks when they suggested linking the number 33 with the Asterix and Obelix comic inspired deed of jumping into the sea with a weight tied to the ankles.

# BOOKING

There are various ways to book a cruise. Those who require attention and guidance should visit a travel agent's. Those who need to hear a human voice, but, as dedicated hypochondriacs, wish to avoid direct contact, should resort to the telephone. Those who are au fait with modern technology and blessed with much patience should consult the internet. And finally those who are not easily parted from their money should either book very late or very early. As diverse as the booking options are the prices prospective buyers pay for exactly the same trip. Discounts can be had for early booking, last minute booking, regular customers, the curious, frequent travellers, honeymoon couples, pensioners, students, families with or without children, divorcees and non-swimmers.

And all of them find themselves accidentally sharing the same table towards the end of the voyage. Instead of enjoying the trip until its harmonious end, some killjoy introduces the subject of the fare. Now we can observe something like a reverse auction where everyone wants to underbid each other. Passengers who've already been beaten in the underbidding war and had to abandon any hope of victory will at least know somebody among their circle of friends and acquaintances who paid even less (far less). At this stage the prevalent mood, except the winner's, has hit rock bottom. If you now want to really add to the general misery and wipe the self-satisfied smirk off the winner's face, you should make your exit with the devastating words: "Well, we forked out 499 quid for the fortnight and I wouldn't have spent a penny more." When you soon after hear a dull splat, the first competitor has voluntarily vacated the ship.

# BOW THRUSTER

The bow thruster is a propeller in a vessel's lower bow, i.e. at the front. It's located right behind the nose, conveniently below the waterline and enables the ship to move sideways. It is also immensely helpful when docking and the envy of many a motorist confronted with a tricky parking spot. How many, if any, bow thrusters a ship is equipped with can easily be discerned by the signs on the bow. The sign for the additional screw propellers is a circle with a cross. If you notice one or several of these when boarding your cruise ship and shortly after move into a cabin at the front, you can safely toss your alarm clock into the ocean. Because on the days your ship is scheduled to enter a port you'll be woken by precisely these bow thrusters at about half past six in the morning.

Using them to ease docking unfortunately entails quite a bit of vibration at the prow. But this doesn't last forever. Unless your mobile hotel anchors off an island such as Santorini (also see Islands) where the cliffs are so steep that the anchor cable has soon reached its limits. So to keep the vessel in position in stormy weather, the bow thrusters are deployed – sometimes all day long. Cabins (also see Cabins) located close to them or the main propellers are preferably assigned to guest entertainers or other inferior voyagers. The crew therefore refers to these unfortunate sub-humans as being screwed.

The noise and vibrations do, however, frequently cause some excitement amongst the passengers. Although the vibrations can be sexually quite diverting, the ordinary guest rarely believes them to be an additional service laid on for newly smitten couples. Conjecture about the commotion's cause is actually far more fanciful – and not just among anxious passengers whose initial suspicion is always that there's something wrong.

The layman likes to imagine piston seizure in an overheated diesel engine. More optimistic guests rule out a defect and speculate quite inventively about an outside source. There is, for instance, the famous helicopter returning the crew in the morning (which, naturally, slept on the mainland). Strangely enough, one never hears the chopper in the night when it allegedly collects the crew. One can only surmise they considerately use gliders so as not to disturb the guests during the small hours. Another hot contender is the idea of construction work in progress close to the cruise ship. It is, after all, quite probable that a just-in-case replacement vessel is being built on a floating dock adjacent to one's own ship and that the building site is cunningly disguised by enormous sea blue nets during the day. Applying the same logic, it is also reasonable to assume that at sea, just like on land, construction works start at half six in the morning with a deafening racket and then cease for the rest of the day. The most ingenious reason, however, was supplied by a technically gifted gentleman who had watched the ship's berthing manoeuvre and noticed the churned up water at the bow. He proudly proceeded to explain to everyone on board that whenever a cruise ship enters a port, the water level in the harbour basin is quickly lowered to accommodate the ocean giant and that the noise stems from colossal pumps.

All these attempted explanations are nevertheless more endearing than the immediate complaints to the shipping line over a disturbed night's rest - a favourite among passengers who love cruises as long as they are not inconvenienced by the vessel itself. First lawsuits from this specific group against the sea per se and its stupid movements have already been successfully dismissed

# BRIDGE

The bridge is the ship's command centre. This is where all the navigating happens and the officers on duty still scan the waters for potential hazards through their binoculars despite the unbelievably high-tech on-board equipment. The term "bridge" was coined more than a century ago when the two wheel housings on the left and right of the good old Mississippi steamboats were connected by a bridge to afford a better view of the considerable traffic on the "Ol' Man River". The system was adopted by other, later vessels without paddle wheels.

The bridge, just like the engine room (also see Engine Room), is one of the most coveted places for many of the male passengers who'd simply love to turn the big wheel or push the big lever to send the full speed ahead, ring-ring signal to the engine. And this is where fantasy and reality collide. The big wheel has yielded to the joystick and the ring-ring lever has been replaced by a significantly smaller one without the ring-ring. Other than that the bridge is jam-packed with the most state-of-the-art navigation technology. Furthermore, every technical process aboard can be viewed on the bridge via monitors. The bridge is quite similar to a spaceship and the only one missing is a cynical gentleman with pointed ears.

An area which often inspires confusion is the bridge wing. This is the bit which extends outwards over the ship's sides. In modern vessels it is usually integrated into the bridge; in older ones it is rather more like a balcony and therefore visible to everyone. The bridge wing includes a smaller control unit that enables the Captain to steer the ship from there when docking due to the enhanced view. It's quite like being able to get out of your car while reverse parking.

When a vigilant passenger once spotted the Captain with two of his staff members on the bridge wing during a docking manoeuvre, he felt neglected by the ship's commanding officers during that precarious moment and was instantly motivated to write a letter of complaint. In his epistle he suggested the Captain choose a more appropriate moment for a little natter with his colleagues and their mutual admiration of the landscape. One nearly expected the writer to finish his outpourings by offering his wife's assistance with directions during the docking process, something the good woman had apparently acquired some experience of with her husband, judging by the type of complaint. Another grievance was based on a simple misunderstanding of the term bridge. Recently an amicable Captain enthusiastically talked to a female voyager about entering the port of Lisbon the following morning. Her question of where he would be at that time he answered truthfully with: "On the bridge." The next morning the woman went on deck to witness the occasion. Shortly before reaching the port, the vessel passed under a huge suspension bridge. Although she unsuccessfully scanned the entire bridge for any sign of the Captain, she wrote a letter of complaint to the cruise line remarking that it would be far safer if the ship's commander remained on board during such a tricky entry instead of viewing his liner from above. The captain vowed to make amends.

## CABIN

One recognises a cruise novice by his embarrassing mistake of referring to the cabin as his "room". Right away cruise pros regard him with pity and it is only with extreme effort that he can gain a position among the illus-trious circle of informed guests.

In days of yore the ship's sleeping quarters were also called cabins, but were hardly comparable to the modern variety and rather like slightly more com-fortable dog kennels. Cabins on modern cruise ships have to be highly effective and provide a maximum of luxury in a minimum of space. The biggest problem when designing and constructing a cabin is just that: the limited space. Were it structurally feasible, one would undoubtedly build very long, extremely nar-row ships to accommodate as many outside cabins as possible. The advantage of outside cabins is that they have windows, ideally even a balcony, and therefore daylight. Which also explains the disadvantage of in-side cabins: the lack of daylight. For the inside cabin passenger it is therefore imperative to wear a watch with a 24-hour dial; otherwise it may easily happen that after a little nap the guest gets dolled up for din-ner at half past six in the morning and unexpectedly encounters the cleaning staff, but no fellow voyag-ers. This and similar downsides of inside cabins have opened many a long married couple's eyes as to how little they actually know each other (also see Marital Crisis).

Should you be the occupant of an inside cabin who would prefer an outside cabin, there is a simple trick to remedy the situation. Some outside cabins have a direct view of an accessible deck like the embarkation deck from where the lifeboats (also see Lifeboats) are boarded. Once you've found such a cabin, and it also appeals to you in terms of layout and furnishings, grab a comfortable deckchair, park yourself outside the cabin's window and take an active interest in what's happening inside. Granted, this requires a little patience, but experience has shown that most outside cabin residents will give up no later than Day 4 and voluntarily offer to swap with you. Should you also be running out of cash, put the desperate occupant off a while longer and only agree on Day 5 against payment of a small fee.

Some tight-fisted cruisaders take a calculated risk and intentionally book a lower priced inside cabin on a ship where the average guest is well into his nineties. Chances are that one or several of the geriatrics won't make it to the end of the cruise and our penny-pinching voyager is upgraded to a more luxuries cabin (with balcony).

Naturally quite a few resourceful passengers have contemplated how to enhance inside cabins. Suggestions range from fitting them with balconies to equipping them with a barbecue area. Also remarkable was the proposal of the amateur inventor who wanted to develop a type of periscope which would enable inside cabin dwellers to observe what's taking place on the lido deck, for instance, via a sophisticated mirror system. Sadly, this basically ingenious idea was stopped by the ship designer's petty objection that roughly 200 periscopes jutting out from the lido deck floor would greatly limit the space for deckchairs. The inventor then

resorted to a less complicated alternative, went upstairs
and had a look.

.

# CAPTAIN

The Captain is the undisputed sovereign of the cruise ship, roughly equivalent to similarly exalted positions like Senior Medical Consultant, President of the United States, Pope etc. Whatever he commands is law, whatever he utters is true; there is nothing he does not know. If a crew member is asked to see the Captain, this rarely implies a pleasant chat over a cup of tea. For that reason the bridge is located high up so that the summoned offender can contemplate his sins on the way.

On a cruise ship the Captain is not only the nautical commander-in-chief, he also performs social duties. The undoubted, the absolute and aloof ruler on the bridge, he has to be approachable when mingling with the guests. Luckily, he can still choose who can touch him and for how long, but he cannot avoid posing for photos with the guests or performing various greeting and farewell ceremonies and welcoming speeches.

The origins of the Captain's Dinner can be traced back to the early 19th century when passengers had to provide their own food. Unfavourable weather conditions frequently prolonged the North Atlantic crossing and the passengers ran out of grub. To preserve the steamship companies' reputation, their owners instructed the captains to serve some of the ships' rations to the starving voyagers. Henceforth this became known as the Captain's Dinner, a tradition which survives to this day, albeit the crew's miserable fare has been replaced by extravagant five course meals.

When the Captain is introduced on stage at the start of the cruise, the amount of cameras flashing suggests that Michael Jackson has risen from the dead and is announcing his comeback. So much adulation is scary. Evidently mature adults go to pieces in His presence and, judging by their body language, are tempted to address Him as Your Highness, Your Excellency or at least in the third person. There are Captains who would then love to reply in the royal we (pluralis majestatis), the way generations of rulers and kings have before them. Undivided attention like this doesn't necessarily agree with everyone and, depending on his inclination, either leads to the Captain constantly basking in his subjects' admiration or spending the least possible amount of time in their company. However, four stripes (also see Stripes) on the shoulder inevitably result in canonisation. The only person on board vaguely approaching the same status is the head chef. But he is more a king of hearts than God incarnate. And in contrast to the head chef the Captain is never cursed when his former passengers weigh themselves once they get home

.

# CHECK-IN

We all know the moment only too well when the Joneses throw a party and greet every guest individually, have a little chat with him and then bestow their undivided attention onto the next arrival. This also happens on The Love Boat. But on modern cruise ships with a capacity of over 5,000 passengers, a welcome like this would take roughly a week. After that one may as well start saying one's goodbyes. The reality is slightly different, but no less interesting. As soon as you arrive at the pier you no longer have to worry about your luggage. Nearly all cruise lines have it delivered straight to your cabin. In most cases it's already taken care of at the airport check-in (very occasionally forever, which isn't necessarily a bad thing as you get to renew your wardrobe at the airline's expense).

The check-in itself usually takes place at the cruise terminal where you can also meet some of the crew members for the first time. Following a short passport and identity screening, you're handed your key card which opens the cabin as well as being a means of payment. Then your hand luggage and you yourself are scanned. The procedure reveals even the tiniest metal bits on your body. People with piercings in intimate places are therefore advised to carry some change in their pockets so they can blame the beeping on the coins without having to blush. Now you can finally enter the ship via the gangway (also see Gangway) to have your photograph taken and be cordially greeted by a commission of dignitaries. And so the holiday really starts – theoretically - because the gods decreed that you have to find your cabin before you start enjoying the cruise. Although the cabin numbers are logically arranged with the first digit identifying the respective deck, and although there are informative direction signs everywhere and friendly staff lurking at every corner, some guests find more or less every room on board, bar their cabin. After the simple instruction "down the hall and then right" they promptly end up in the crew's quarters or the walk-in closet where the cleaning agents are stored. Thus it can happen that one or the other utterly exhausted passenger erring around the staircase way past midnight has to be saved from potential dehydration. But for him, too, the crew is bound to produce a welcome drink. And then, at last, the holiday begins.

# CREW

The crew constitutes the part of the ship's population which has far more fun without the passengers. This claim isn't just unfair, it's also simply wrong. Unfair because there are many crew members on board who downright enjoy dealing with the public, in whatever form. And wrong because the majority of the crew would be redundant without guests and therefore wouldn't qualify as being crew.

To be a crew member is a dream job. At least in the eyes of the passengers. Wouldn't you love to say to an ordinary passenger: "I am part of the crew!" To be on the ship's staff is enviable to the extent that numerous cruisaders, by the second last day at the latest, would gladly forego their hefty paycheque and swap places with the crew – because for the crew the holiday never ends. Which is basically most of the guests' general idea: being crew means being on a permanent vacation. Well, that's not quite true. Although it is rumoured that some crew members spend their shore leave on board, the work on a cruise ship isn't all unadulterated joy. The crew's quarters are cramped and you can't just take a quick trip into town whenever you fancy. You can't even have a little stroll around the garden. You live in extremely crowded conditions for a relatively long period. If you don't have the nerve for that, you'll soon suffer from extreme claustrophobia.

How little the guests know about the crew is constantly revealed by interesting questions such as: "Does the crew also sleep on-board?" – "No, of course not. *The Queen Mary 2* is right behind us and we're ferried over every night." As absurd and actually impertinent this reply may be, some guests subsequently scan the horizon with their binoculars and some of them are convinced they've spotted the *QM2's* blurred outlines in the distance.

But every passenger should be clear about one thing: some areas on-board are reserved for the crew only. On the one hand the respective liner's luxurious ambience is reduced to a shocking minimum in the staff quarters, a minimum one couldn't expect a passenger to put up with. On the other, the crew also has a right to leisure time, preferably even without the guests. At this point the adventures of an unaccompanied gentleman should be mentioned who, highly inebriated, tried to find shelter in various crew members' bunks and had to be escorted back to his cabin by security. The next day he tried to talk his way out by claiming he read "Crew lonely" instead of "Crew only" on the signs in the staff quarters and compassionately attempted to remedy the situation.

.

# D

## DARDANELLES

The Dardanelles are a strait between the European peninsula of Gallipoli and Turkey, Anatolia, to be precise. The strait connects the Aegean See with the Sea of Marmara. From there it's an easy trip from Istanbul via the Bosporus to the Black Sea. This strategically important route was fiercely fought over for centuries. Cruises, however, rarely include it in their itinerary in the hope of taking part in an exciting naval battle but because of its proximity to the historically significant Troy. Which brings us to the historical event of epic proportions which still baffles the more learned: why would anyone in full command of their senses want to annoy the Spartans, a species of warrior not exactly for the faint-hearted?

And seeing that the ship is now really close to the Aegean Sea with its numerous islands, Ephelides, Basorexia and Pica are not among their number, but are respectively an abundance of freckles, the overwhelming desire to kiss and the compulsion to eat inedible objects.

# DECK

The word deck derives from the late Middle English "dekke" (via Middle Dutch), meaning to cover. Later on it evolved into describing a solid surface. The first known vessels were not covered and over time man realised it would be wise to put something over the cargo to protect it from the elements and built the first decks. A cruiser has an abundance of them, so-called tween (from in between) decks, a bit like storeys in a house. The word deck also belongs to those a seasoned cruise enthusiast should add to his vocabulary in order to denote his affiliation with the world of seafaring folk. The most famous kind of deck must be the sun deck. The name indicates its purpose. On a fine day it seems as if the passengers on a cruise ship view sunbathing as a mandatory exercise. On these occasions the sun deck resembles a busy Mediterranean beach at the height of season. Only the beach is missing. But the lido deck makes up for it. For that reason the sun deck is also called lido deck (also see Lido Deck).

With a little common sense one can match most of the decks with their purpose. The promenade deck (predecessor of the sun deck) dates back to the era of the Titanic, when one didn't yet bask shamelessly, half naked in the sun. Promenading, in other words taking a leisurely stroll, fulfilled a function comparable to step aerobics with conversation, albeit people back then weren't quite as quickly out of breath.

The bridge deck is where the bridge is (also see Bridge) and the main deck's location is also quite obvious. But then it gets tricky. The spar deck, contrary to popular belief, is not the part of the vessel intended for amateur pugilists or the place where warring lovers can vent their frustration. It is either synonymous with the upper deck or a deck above the cargo holds. Easily confused also is the wonderfully named poop deck, which is not what you might think, but forms the roof of a cabin at the stern. And, anyhow, baked beans are not exactly standard fare on a cruise ship menu.

# DECKCHAIRS

On German cruise ships the deckchairs on the lido deck are not only THE object of desire, securing them also most impressively illustrates German efficiency and strategic skills. The Teutonic race not only excels in the production of beer, sausages and lederhosen, it also invented the concept of deckchair reservation. To be on the safe side, most cruise ships carrying a large proportion of German tourists therefore ask their guests not to reserve their deckchairs and to "release" them again after a prolonged absence. Some ships also tried to introduce "deckchair wardens" who left notes deliberately designed to resemble parking tickets on unoccupied yet reserved deckchairs after a certain amount of time had elapsed. The guests gratefully acknowledged the entertaining gesture but stoically clung to their tried and tested custom. Would Mr Porsche ever have driven a Ferrari? Would Mr Frankfurter have ever eaten a Hamburger? Absolutely not! By the same token one can't expect the brain behind the concept of deckchair reservation to adopt alien customs and to forego his very own invention. Quite the contrary. Pride in the patent keeps engendering innovative improvements in the field of rationally planned sunbathing.

The sun doesn't stay in the one place is how the fact that the earth circles this bright star is generally described. Thus the needy deckchair reserver requires not only ONE place in the sun but several. And thanks to the ample supply of towels (also see Towels) on board, the endeavour to reserve those only requires a minimum of extra effort. Besides, there is the worry about skin cancer. Here, too, the seasoned reserver has made his provisions and secured more than one shady spot, carefully taking the sun's position into account.

Youth's privilege is the ignorance of the traditional – and sleeping a lot as well as partying even more. It therefore sometimes happens that young people enjoy their final nightcap on deck at the same time as the first reservers are on patrol. This naturally incites adolescent rebels to revolt against the established order and throw all the towels into the pool. One should neither welcome nor condemn such juvenile hotheads' excesses, but should remember that the Thirty Years' War started for far more trivial reasons.

# DRAUGHT

The biggest draught of any cruise ship is currently (still) that of the *Queen Mary* 2 with close to 34 feet. But otherwise it is endeavoured to keep the draught, i.e. the amount of space the vessel occupies beneath the waterline, as small as possible as many ports have already reached their limits and cannot be dredged any further without hitting upon the first magma chambers. Even when the cruise line accepts that their vessel can't enter a port but has to anchor off the coast, shallow banks near the shore may also put certain restrictions to this. Apart from that it may only be possible to anchor outside the three mile zone and operate tender services (also see Tender) in excess of three hours long. So much about the depth problem beneath the water.

Quite another is the depth problem above the water. Some flippantly claim that the passengers' intellectual depth is in inverse proportion to the ship's draught. In other words: the more depth a vessel draws, the more shallow its occupants' conversations. This is, however, quite a frivolous assertion as philosophical discussions have been overheard on the *QM*2 (34 feet draught) and chitchat about digestive problems on the *Europa* (19 feet). This means the guests (and not the ship) are responsible for their intellectual depth. Yet another example of the consumer having to increasingly draw on his own resources, but also an inevitable development in an age where one has to assemble one's own flat pack furniture.

## ENGINE ROOM

On a cruise liner the engine room is usually found on Deck 2, i.e. nearly all the way down, beneath the waterline. For male passengers it holds an enormous erotic appeal. Given the choice, the average male would rather have a peep at the engine room than spent the night with Scarlett Johansson. This may also be due to the fact that since September 11 this Holy of Holies is far less publicly accessible on most ships.

And yet having a glance at the engine room is about as exciting as looking under the bonnet of the Ford Focus 2010 model. One sees – nothing. Or nearly nothing. Because the little there is to see is neatly hidden behind metal housings, nicely painted in fashionable pastel shades of aquamarine blue or light lapis lazuli. No oil, no rattling valves, no steam, no sweaty operators who notice from the sound alone which of the 16 pistons has just experienced lubricant loss for a fraction of a second. The mentally unstable Chief Mechanic Johann from the German cult classic *Das Boot* (also released as *Das Boot* in English) has become redundant. Johann's replacement generally has a Japanese-German name, four processors and everything under control. Also gone are the days described in Fellini's classic And the Ship Sails on where eccentric opera singers regale the marvelling stokers with a special concert against the background of blazing flames emanating from open boiler doors. Romance has given way to prosaic technology. And still, a pleasant shiver runs down the spine of any man who, against all the odds, makes it into the room of his desires. Apparently just the thought of the incredible 30,000 HP is enough for the rapt spectator. But eventually it all ends like the night with Scarlett Johansson when the imagination surpasses reality.

# ENTERTAINMENT

A cruise ship will always lay on lots of entertainment as many of its guests are not satisfied merely gazing at the sea or the buffet for long periods of time. What's on offer greatly varies depending on the ship and your budget – anything from spectacular shows, some of them even on ice, right down to the magician one otherwise only encounters at kids' birthday parties. So-called walking acts sometimes provide spontaneous, small-scale diversion when least expected. Here one or two comedians amaze with funny capers which make the guests chuckle or send them straight to reception (also see Reception) to complain. It would be less confusing if those actors wore a badge saying: "We're only joking." But they don't. Therefore stunts like "blatant bimbo hits on husband at check-in" or "phoney ship's doctor doles out Viagra" are often misinterpreted and result in grievances being aired.

On international ships this doesn't happen or only rarely. Because here the language barrier has created a natural boundary. On French ships people speak French, on American ships they speak English but on international ones – like Italian liners, for example – they speak everything. Simultaneously or successively. Thus it can happen that the introductions to a variety show in English, French, Italian, German and Japanese take so long that the first tired guests already retire to their cabin before the actual entertainment starts. Even entering the picturesque port of Curacao accompanied by a narration in five languages can take so long that, despite the interesting little Lego houses lining its sides, the last of those languages is only heard when the vessel is about to depart again.

But all this bears witness to the fact that most cruise lines invest heavily in their guests' entertainment to prevent their human cargo from boring each other to tears.

# ETIQUETTE

Etiquette can be defined as a rule of conduct applicable to certain social circles such as a cruise ship's clientele. To this day this includes the dress code on traditional ships like the *Queen Mary 2*. If the first evening is a formal black tie event, the correct or incorrect attire labels its wearer and determines his social standing for the rest of the cruise. But etiquette has become quite relaxed on the more package deal oriented cruises. The galas, Captain's dinners and balls are now conducted in a more casual manner which renders wearing a tuxedo unnecessary. But, as usually happens in real life, as soon as the established rules are abolished, anarchy rears its ugly head. Inhibitions disappear and shorts or tracksuit bottom clad rumps make their appearance in the restaurants (also see Restaurant). Fortunately, the trend of attending the buffet dripping wet, wrapped in a towel after the sauna, could be stopped just in time. When you're constantly told to make yourself feel at home, the temptation to do just that is understandable. Yet considering the way some passengers present themselves on-board, one would rather be kept in the dark as to what their homes look like.

One can easily discern early childhood damages from a passenger's behaviour without having to engage the services of a psychologist:

People who sit down to dinner without greeting their fellow diners and proceed to commandeer most of the available space certainly had to fight for their position in the family hierarchy during infancy.

Hiking sandals and long toenails reveal an upbringing near the equator combined with the need of maintaining a firm grip when clinging to tall trees.

Monosyllable orders directed at the staff without the troublesome "please" or "thank you" arise from an unfulfilled early childhood desire for a vocational orientation in the direction of top management.

As one can see: even those who don't adhere to the remaining bit of etiquette that should be observed aboard a cruise ship can at least add to the general entertainment.

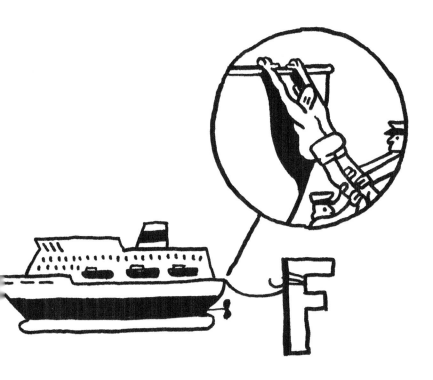

## FAREWELL

All good things must come to an end and so must even
the most beautiful, in fact even the longest cruise. If
you don't happen to spend the last day in the laundrette (also see Laundrette) for a final wash of your
travel outfits and have a good ponder instead whilst
wistfully gazing out to sea, you'll soon be overcome by

ever growing parting pains. And it is looming: the fare-well from the ship, from the crew, from new friends, the little jar before lunch, dancing the night away, titillating flirtations and, of course, from the ocean itself. In a nutshell, saying your goodbyes to the best part of the year. By the time the sun goes down one can thus observe more and more passengers indulging in their sweet sorrow with a pretend blissful expression while forcefully trying to repeatedly prolong the finality of this, the last day. If they have so far not wasted any thoughts on the volley ball team, they suddenly watch their matches with rapture and decide to join the athletic gang on their next cruise. If they previously could hardly wait for the sun to make its exit so they could finally take a shower, they now abide on deck until darkness falls, still hoping the sun may change its mind just for once and make another appearance.

These collective parting pangs are also hard for the crew to ignore, even if they usually entertain entirely different thoughts about possibly returning home. And as it is always delightful to wallow in a shared emotion, the sentiment is so elaborately milked with schmaltzy farewell entertainment and parties on the last night on board, every passenger subsequently feels that the crew will be deeply depressed after his departure. This would most probably be true if the next guests didn't embark just minutes later to be greeted with the same euphoria as those about to leave had been only a few days earlier. Thus depression is solely reserved for the departing guests who can either drown their sorrows in vast amounts of alcohol or temporarily suppress their misery by attempting to hide somewhere unnoticed. But even the latter will sooner or later be carried off the ship screaming and kicking to make room for the next guests who are already doomed to experience the same fate by the end of their cruise.

# FJORDS

A popular cruise destination are the beauties of the Norwegian fjords. These estuaries, which extend far into the mainland, were created by glacial erosion during the last ice age.

In fine weather and for those blessed with a stable psyche, the Geiranger and Hardanger fjords amongst others are well worth a visit. When the sun shines, they are sensational: white clouds are mirrored in unfathomable depths, foaming water searches for a path to freedom from mysterious cliffs with sparse vegetation and creates wonderful formations of waterfalls with gently emerging rainbows. But woe betide him who chooses a trip through the fjords to overcome a personal, presently extremely depressing existential crisis and, to top it all, the weather is bad. He is destined for even more doom and gloom. Black clouds don't get reflected on black, infinitely deep waters. The bleak rock faces to the left and right of the ship are rarely relieved – by grey waterfalls. In addition the staff tries to sweeten the melancholic atmosphere by playing sombre symphonies composed by suicidal artists such as Grieg or Alvorsen. Quite often the mulled wine served in the morning on entering the fjord to prepare for the associated sudden drop in temperature quickly results in the blues replacing the initial euphoria experienced by many a voyager.

But every fjord eventually ends inland and everyone looks forward to stepping ashore to mix with the jaunty Norwegians and escape from the misery. The quaint alleyways and colourful timber houses radiate warmth and cosiness. As they have to because it can get not just unpleasantly dismal but also extremely cold in the summer as well.

Even the most spectacular midnight sun doesn't do anything to alleviate matters when it bashfully hides behind grey clouds. Particularly the northern parts of the country experience the occasional winter in the midst of summer. But when the season actually corresponds to the calendar once in a while, the Norwegian fjords are among the most beautiful places on this planet and highly recommended. There's only one minor drawback that badly affects the above mentioned suicidal mood: even the most powerful satellite dishes have no reception between the spectacularly high cliffs and the passenger stranded without phone, internet and TV may just have to read a book to divert himself. Which doesn't necessarily have to be a work by the Norwegian dramatist Ibsen with the cheerful title *When We Dead Awaken!*

## GALLEY

In the days when one still scraped the mould from the ship's biscuits in this place, the galley was called a caboose. Some form of mush, as filling as possible, was cooked here or putrid water boiled to make it somewhat palatable again. That's no longer the case – the thing about the water. Only kidding, the same applies to the food.

The galleys on cruise liners are state-of-the-art industrial kitchens with a heat-resistant team of creative gourmet chefs who magically produce hundreds of delicacies every day, seven days a week, without a break. To this end they use tons of ingredients which are kept in fridges, freezers, dry stores and cold rooms managed by the provision master. Granted, this logistical tour de force may perhaps also be observed at her Majesty's Revenue and Customs office canteen, but logistics are just one challenge. Location is quite another. It is common knowledge that the galley is located on the ship itself and not suspended by a clever gyro system which counteracts most of the sway. The rocking to and fro the passengers perceive as unpleasant when the sea is rough can also be felt in the galley. This does occasionally relieve the need to stir whatever is cooking on the hi-tech hobs, but it's quite a challenge to write with icing on a wedding cake when the waves are thirty feet high. "Congratulations, Wanda and Sylvester" can thus easily turn into: "Congr u Wa ster!

# GANGWAY

This peculiar chicken ladder like contraption, used to board or leave the ship, is called a gangway. Depending on the landing pier and the water level in the harbour basin, the gangway can be affixed to different parts of the ship and at varying heights. This poses the first problem. Once the average cruisader has become accustomed to a certain exit to the mainland and heads for it despite several announcements that the exit is now located elsewhere and finds himself facing locked doors, he feels baffled and disorientated. Many a time when passengers embark on land excursions, totally dehydrated and desperate individuals, who unsuccessfully tried to leave the vessel, were discovered in the evening. Only with difficulty, and after several hours in the infirmary, could they be reunited with the merry flock of more enlightened guests.

Although most liners have their own gangway, on occasion the gangway is on temporary loan from the respective port. In this case it can happen that the model is a bit on the narrow side. "So what?" will be the response of the more sprightly voyager in his sixties, who is delighted that he can now hold on to both sides. But it's not quite as simple as that when a lot of passengers with Zimmer frames leave the ship at the same time or want to get back on board after a rather short trip ashore. The main problem is that the international maritime organisations still haven't devised a definite code of conduct for instances like this. And as the average Zimmer frame driver also rarely possesses the necessary patience, uproar develops at the foot, the top or in the middle of the gangway where the Zimmer frame users not only infrequently hurl abuse at each other but also engage in physical combat. As much as one marvels at the pensioners' spontaneous agility, which is close to a biblical miracle ending with the words "I can walk again!", one just as much fears the sequel with the exclamation "I can throw a punch again!" And as much as the waiting passenger has cursed those cumbersome walking aids, one quickly realises their major advantage when compared to ordinary crutches. Although, in contrast to the Zimmer frame, the aforementioned don't cause as much gridlock, they can also be more readily deployed as a weapon.

# GUESTS

In the olden days civilians travelling on a ship were simply called "passengers", a highly appropriate and suitable term seeing that these people had merely booked a passage from A to B. The accommodation provided was either a suite with a butler or a spot in the dormitories amongst the other plebs. A cruise, however, isn't simply a passage between A and B, but more like a sightseeing tour of various ports and their environs. Therefore one could probably get away with calling the travellers "tour-ists". But because most of today's passengers are cordially invited, they are referred to as guests. The cruise companies have adopted the idea of an invitation from Yorkshire peasant weddings where one also has to contribute a lot of dosh to be included in the party.

Guests are basically nice, as is apparent from the way they are addressed. Even when they're not so nice at times, they are still addressed as "dear guests". But should guests not only not be nice but downright rude, which often happens on a cruise, they are esteemed. This is merely due to the fact that the appeasing staff member's tongue would rot in his mouth had he to say "dear guest" whereas "esteemed guest" kind of inspires a feeling of indifference.

Incidentally, just like for the crew, there is also a career ladder for the passengers to climb. The lowest rung is occupied by the novices; those who are taking a cruise for the first time AND also for the first time on this particular ship. Half a rung higher up are those who have at least been on a cruise before, regardless of the destination. Then there are the so-called repeaters with two or more journeys on this vessel or type of vessel under their belts. At the very top are those who consider themselves to be part of the ship's interior based on their extensive cruising history. These highly decorated cruisaders are also the most difficult from the crew's perspective and comparable to party guests who raid your fridge uninvited, run a bath for themselves and end up having a nap in your bed. They also no longer bother to reserve any deck chairs, but store "their" loungers in their cabins to simplify matters. When chatting to the crew they'll occasionally ask: "By the way, how long have you been working for us?" But these long-term inmates get their facts mixed up. The only ones who are permitted to act like that on a cruise are not the guests but the actual owners of the ship.

## HOSPITAL

Every cruise ship has a hospital with real doctors and real nurses. Because cruise operators also spare no expense when selecting these staff members, the physicians are usually distinguished authorities in their field. As such quite a few cruisaders embark on the journey purely motivated by the medical treatment options. Particularly among the more difficult patients with heretofore unexplored ailments there is a trend towards on-board treatment tourism where top diagnosticians are already traded on the internet.

Ship's doctors, with or without a celebrity halo, are universally adored and, on account of their numerous female fans, only venture to the bar in the company of a bodyguard. More often than not this is someone with four stripes on the shoulders of his uniform (also see Captain) who is the only man on board who can temporarily divert the ladies' attention away from the good doctor.

A sick bay on a cruise ship has to be prepared for every eventuality. Even minor surgical procedures. This does not only concern the passengers who broke a finger when snapping it too hard at bingo (also see Bingo) but also possible accidents involving the hard working crew. Once again American cruise liners outshine all others with their excesses. Where many European ships already have their own dialyses machine to cater for renal disease sufferers, American liners are equipped with every conceivable medical appliance and gadget. Their infirmaries are truly gigantic and nothing is impossible – from life-cell therapy using herring embryos to organ transplants and plastic surgery. Some say there are guests who had to be accompanied by their attending physician on re-entering their native country because their appearance differed too greatly from that of their passport photo before the voyage.

The hospital also includes the on-board dispensary where headache pills and condoms feature in top place on the list of required items and are often purchased in that combination. This naturally gives rise to the question why they're doing it so much if they always get a headache afterwards? But this question is only rarely asked.

## ISLANDS

Be it in the Caribbean or the Mediterranean (also see Mediterranean), islands are always a favourite cruise destination. Many a tranquil isle presents the voyagers with an illusion of paradise. The smallest of them (the islands not the voyagers) have adjusted to the boom by now and are extending their port facilities accordingly while consistently lagging behind trying to accommodate the vessels' vast dimensions and the speed at which they are being built.

Even the tiniest islands aren't spared from tourist invasions. At popular destinations the ships often have to line up before the island to unleash the flood of sightseers onto its population on tenders (also see Tender). At peak season up to ten ocean liners may thus be anchored at the coast and the number of expectant visitors far exceeds that of the locals. It has already been considered if it would be more expedient to invite the island dwellers on board for lunch for reasons of sustainability and to further the cultural exchange. But protesting guests soon put a stop to that, their main argument being that they had, after all, paid for full board and lodgings, not culture. Safety at the lunch buffet and missing souvenirs were also a major issue and therefore the idea was quickly discarded.

Very special is the island of Santorini. This blue-white gem of the Southern Cyclades must surely be the most remarkable Greek isle and is actually an archipelago like those in the South Pacific. Countless volcanic eruptions have created impressive coastal cliffs with those famous, extraordinarily picturesque small fishing villages on top. A sight not to be missed. But how does one get to them? The cliffs are up to 900 feet high and the sea below them nearly 270 fathoms deep. As already mentioned, tenders take the willing cruisader to one of the little harbours. Now one only has to tackle the cliffs. To this end one can either hop onto the hopelessly overburdened cable car or, at the risk of falling, climb up an overpopulated path on one's own feet or on someone else's feet – a donkey's. Several hundred donkeys, well, actually their drivers, bravely offer their services to deliver the sightseers to the top. Santorini is, however, also a much loved destination of American cruise ships. Without meaning to promote prejudices, it is an unavoidable fact that the United States are the birthplace of the Hamburger. To this day, the disastrous long-term effects are sadly observable in quite a few Americans and the average Northern European, as so often, gladly follows in their footsteps. When these morbidly obese creatures mount one of the poor donkeys or, more accurately, are heaved onto it, the animal slightly sags, but courageously soldiers on although mostly obscured by its rider's bulk. This may go as far as the traveller's bum cheeks dragging over the ground. After much coaching and the constant feeding of restoratives, both man and beast happily and generally make it up the steep serpentines. Happily? The rider perhaps, but the donkey most certainly not. But nobody ever asks him. In the context of a greater acceptance of other religious persuasions' belief in Karma one wonders what kind of a person somebody must have been to be reborn as a donkey on Santorini. Perhaps an American tourist, which would satisfy a certain amount of cosmic justice

## JUMPING (& FLYING) FISH

Because a cruise is usually conducted on an ocean liner and not a glass-bottomed submarine, the abundant marine life, apart from the ever popular dolphins and whales, is sadly only rarely seen – with the exception of their imaginatively prepared remains at the buffet or in the restaurant. All the greater is the general commotion when the first flying fish jump out of the water in the more southerly climates. It usually takes a couple of minutes until some especially astute passengers comprehend that they're witnessing something they had hitherto only known from the realm of legends. Before long, amazement is accompanied by a fear of the unknown. "What if those slippery creatures land on board or attack us?" The prevalent excitement soon escalates into a wave of hysteria where every individual passenger already imagines the tabloid headline: "Attack of the flying killer fish – several casualties!"

This fear is not as unfounded as it may seem. Since the heavy flooding in the southern states of America in the 1990s, "jumping fish" have been sighted on the Mississippi. However, they are not a species of flying fish but are, in fact, a variety of Asian carps which eat practically everything alive on the river. Frightened by the noise of boat engines, they leap out of the water and numerous people have been severely injured by collisions with them. Be that as it may, it is highly unlikely that a cruise ship will take the wrong turn at the Gulf of Mexico and end up on the Mississippi.

A little excursion into the world of marine biology may help at this point. Flying fish can't actually fly; they can only glide. Fleeing from their predators, they go full throttle, jump out of the water and spread their oversized pectoral fins. They then glide for a few yards before plunging back into the water in the hope that their enemy has lost track of them. Naturally, now and then one of these panic mongers involuntarily ends up in a rowing boat, but to reach the 60 foot high sun deck would require an extremely powerful, turbo driven gust of wind. The fear of flying fish thus has its origin in a naïve ignorance of the marine fauna which found its pinnacle in the following little episode.

Two men, leaning across the railing, were discussing the unexpected ecological awareness of the port of Isla Margerita over a beer and talked shop about the suction robot which was in the process of cleaning the dock. They were particularly mesmerised by the invisible power supply and controls of the high-tech appliance which turned out to be a stunning, and stunned, lost manta ray. In the gentlemen's defence it needs to be mentioned that the ray did actually leave clear traces of filtered water behind. What the ray did, however, filter from the water instead of plankton, is perhaps better left unexplored. But overall cruise passengers' marine biology knowledge never ceases to amaze: hardly anyone would mistake herring fillets for swordfish steaks at the buffet and nearly everyone knows the difference between tuna nigiri and salmon sushi.

## KIDS

"Children bring joy to the home" or something like that, as the old Siamese (now Thailand) saying goes. "To the home", it says; "on board" doesn't get a mention. Kids are, however, always welcome on board. So welcome that shipping lines do everything in their power to separate them as quickly and as effectively as possible from the other guests. Thus most cruises offer dedicated kids-only zones, child minders, kids-only meals, excursions to child friendly beaches or adventure parks and on-board entertainment for and with kids. In short, the little ones are meant to have a fantastic time, fantastic enough that their parents can enjoy a few days without constantly being run off their feet minding the little monsters – which also applies to the rest of the guests. So parents (and other travellers) fully appreciate how lucky they are to have their offspring professionally looked after, the nippers are occasionally unleashed on the guests. Dressed up as pirates (also see Pirates) they are allowed to advertise their forthcoming show at the on-board theatre and take full advantage of the occasion. Following a generous amount of time allocated to them in demographically authentic surroundings, the average guest is quite happy when the brats are locked up again for the rest of the day.

The kids' self-promotion does, however, appeal to post-menopausal ladies on the far side of 50 whose biological clocks have ceased ticking because their batteries gave up their ghosts long ago. Thus they attend the kids' performance at the theatre, with or without spouse, where they delight in the youngsters' gormless antics on the stage. Yet one has to admit that these shows are actually quite entertaining and amusing even for people without parental pride in their issue and the desperate need to reproduce.

Parents quickly get wind of the available and attentive all-round care for their offspring and so it ever more frequently happens that doting mums and dads enquire at reception where they can drop off their little ones before they've even checked into their cabin. Those parents are then usually very disappointed that their brood is delivered back to them at night. Just as disappointed are parents who can't pawn off their just about weaned one-year-old to the youngest group catering for kids from three upwards although their toddler "is incredibly advanced for his age". This particular species of parents' eyes glaze over when they hear the warning to please not let the kiddies clamber about the railing. How gladly they would let little Nigel demonstrate how "far advanced" he already is. Should the lad's gymnastic efforts turn out to be not as advanced as expected, they at least won't have to worry about paying for babysitting services anymore.

For quite some time clever ex-cruise ship child minders, who have witnessed incidents like this, have been planning to set up a rescue centre for unwanted holiday kids, like those popular dog boarding kennels. So far they are still impeded by tiresome regulations from the youth welfare services, but in the long run their project is assured of a bright future.

## LADIES' CHOICE

There are men who enjoy dancing. They are admittedly the exception, but some cruise companies take advantage of the fact and engage their services as paid dancing partners. These gentlemen of advanced years differ only marginally from female escorts apart from the fact that they don't have to do any of the stimulating as the ladies already feel stimulated enough at the prospect of shortly being able to dance with one of the species. The extraordinary job of professional dance partner is facilitated by three irrefutable points:

1. men's lower life expectancy as compared to that of the fair sex and the resultant excess of women of a certain age,
2. the frequently large age difference during their lifetimes and
3. the ever-present, already mentioned dancing phobia of the male gender.

These gentlemen, above all present on American cruise liners, are more often than not the main booking reason for lonely, elderly women who'd rather spend their remaining years at bingo (also see Bingo) and the slow waltz than in a nursing home in the suburbs. To be brutally honest, one can't always be sure of one's present location when watching the dancers. The only unmistakable indication that one is not in a nursing home is the slight swaying of the ship.

Even if these "gigolos'" fixed salary appears to be negligible, they can, with a bit of luck, count on inheriting millions from one or the other female acquaintance they made on board. The prospect of late riches presumably makes them forget the oddity of their profession.

# LAUNDRETTE

Nearly all cruise ships have a laundrette. Not just the industrial kind for cleaning the bed linen and the ever dwindling supply of towels (also see Towels), which is still dominated by the Chinese, but also one for the guests. And this is well frequented. Maybe not so much at the outset of the journey, but increasingly so as it progresses and particularly on the last day.

The sun is beaming onto the lido deck, the sea is calm, the breeze is pleasant, flying fish (also see Jumping Fish) sail by, dolphins frolic in the background and the cocktails taste better than ever. Can there be anything more beautiful? Absolutely! For hundreds of proud housewives there is nothing more beautiful than returning home with freshly laundered clothes. And thus the laundrette is a hive of activity on the last day where they all fight over the best washing machines and their turn at the dryer. Meanwhile the less efficient spend their last day idly lounging by the pool.

But the laundrette is also quite busy much earlier on. The first reason for this has to do with disagreements; the second with romance. Not the way you think. The ship is already swaying enough as it is and then there are the bow thrusters (also see Bow Thrusters), so there's no need for ardent couples to pleasure each other on the washing machines as well. No, we mean romance in the real sense of the word. Husbands keen to please their wives want to prove that deep down they are true gentlemen who would actually do anything for their spouses if only their time would permit. Men of every age. You will find those at the laundrette for the first reason (disagreements) after he's so badly fallen out with his better half that she now refuses to wash his dirty socks and underwear. Let him see where he'll be without her!

If you ever want to observe truly desperate faces, spend an afternoon at the laundrette from about Day 6 on where you'll find gentlemen close to a nervous breakdown. For many of them this is the first time they've even seen a washing machine up close. At least that's what it seems like. Grown men in positions of authority, branch managers of mutual savings banks or department heads of medium-sized enterprises are faced with the choice: colour, cotton, synthetics or delicates? 30, 40, 60 or 90 degrees? Prewash, rinse or spin? So much misery in such a confined space is usually only encountered in a shared 120 square feet bachelor flat or at some male self-help groups. Flannel boxer shorts are washed at 90 degrees together with the wife's silk pyjamas. The woollen jumper she knitted with her own fair hands is placed in the dryer for three hours after the hot wash. The previously size XL garment is now roughly the size of a dish cloth from Peppa Pig's toy kitchen. In the end disbelief is accompanied by despair and bewilderment by tears.

But should a woman enter the scene, one of those enlightened beings familiar with the art of doing the laundry, all the men gaze at her starry-eyed and instantly fall in love. The all-knowing creature is as (if not more) welcome as the arrival of the cavalry was for early American settlers being challenged by a bunch of disgruntled red Indians. And never was there a woman in their life who was as beautiful, as clever and as desirable.

# LIDO DECK

The lido deck is, without doubt, a cruise ship's social hub. This is where one meets for communal sun-bathing. Of course, it is far more crowded on the days when the ship doesn't put into harbour somewhere than it is on the days when excursions are on offer. So that the tanning process isn't unduly boring, the ship's entertainment department usually lays on some diversion – from background music to amusing games.

The centre of the lido deck is the pool, occasionally even several of them. Analogous to a solar system, one calls these a poolyverse. Those setting foot on the lido deck for the first time are amazed by the size of the pool which is – small. Really just an oversized bath tub. And this applies to most ocean liners. There are two reasons for this. On the one hand, water moves and can adversely affect the ship's stability. On the other, the pool is situated right on top, at a structurally unfavourable spot. Would it, for instance, be located on Deck 2, one could easily install an Olympic-size swimming pool – but without the sun. Cruise ship designers therefore occasionally compromise by incorporating a counter current system to accommodate exercise enthusiasts. The pool is generally filled with salt water, which is sucked in in its purest form on the open seas, to serve a good cause when being discharged in the evenings: the residue of the care products it contains protects our whale population from the dreaded sunburn when they surface.

One can easily discern the dominant nationality on a lido deck or cruise ship respectively by zooming in with Google Earth. This doesn't even have to be as detailed as being able to read the label on the sunscreen lotion. If the deckchairs are reserved with towels, it is definitely a German ship. When a Google image implies that the vessel is burning because the reddish tints are so pronounced, you are looking at a British ship and whatever is burning are the bodies of the sunburnt Sassenachs. Towards the end of the first day at sea those poor unfortunates have already exhausted the galley's entire yoghurt supplies and aloe-vera lotion prices are at an all-time high. Even satin underwear feels like rusty chainmail and the odd passenger succumbs to a pain-induced coma at the slightest touch.

Every British passenger basically parts with most of his skin over the course of his cruise. From a psychological perspective it isn't necessarily a bad thing to change one's appearance in one fell swoop, but from a medical viewpoint this is a disaster. Particularly cute and entertaining, however, are the guests who, regardless of their nationality, nod off in the sun on their first day at sea, still exhausted from the taxing journey to get to their ship or the equally exhausting pool party (also see Pool Party). Preferably when sitting with their head lowered and their hands placed on their exposed thighs. The charming result is a genteel pale face and cleavage with a sunburnt neck and red thighs with amazingly white hand imprints.

# LIFEBOATS

Good news: every cruise ship has enough lifeboat places to cater for everyone. One just has to find them should the necessity arise. Under international maritime law all passengers have to attend a sea rescue drill (also see Sea Rescue Drill). Yet there are still passengers who apparently don't pay much attention during those drills, which provides the only explanation for the following story.

On many vessels, in order not to unduly waste space, the winches which lower the boats into the water swivel them over the railing so they hang suspended above the disembarkation deck. Passengers can comfortably walk under them and have a good look at their bottoms from underneath. One day a scantily clad guest stormed into the reception located on the same deck where he angrily exclaimed that as much as he understood the need to economise, even for cruise companies, they were going too far on this ship. Particularly on days as hot as today they had an obligation to assure their guests' welfare and it was intolerable that the fans were turned off just to save money. The friendly receptionist stared at him in bewilderment. Fans? Where did he think those fans were? The gentlemen became even more enraged and dangerously close to a heatstroke. Outside, of course, he explained, hanging from the ceilings! Perhaps the woman should have copped on at that stage, but she didn't. Thus the enraged guest pulled her out from behind the counter and onto the disembarkation deck where he had sought shelter from the burning sun – in the shade of the lifeboats. The lifeboats with those nice little propellers at the back. A dedicated member of staff would now have instructed the crew to turn on the six lifeboats' diesel engines and have them running at full throttle for a few hours. But the lady from reception merely enlightened the guest about his little misunderstanding. Witnesses later reported that same said gentlemen had begged for asylum in the galley's cold store.

# M

## MAIDEN VOYAGE

A maiden (or virgin) voyage is not a cruise in paradise to reward Islamic suicide bombers, but simply a
ship's first voyage. Since time immemorial ships are
basically female and even the odd exception with a
male name such as the *Lord of the Glens* or the *Marco
Polo* is referred to as she; ergo all ships are ladies. Any
ship which has never been exposed to the rough seas
is therefore a maiden and no longer a maiden after its
first voyage. But how does a ship lose its virginity? Is
it by people climbing aboard or, even worse, by soiling
it? Or could it be nautical expressions like "raising the
mast", "entering the harbour" and "at the helm" that

in a perverted imagination deny the ship the right to prolonged virginity? Anyway, maiden voyages enjoy a virtually unbeatable level of appeal.

Being a passenger on a maiden voyage is in such demand among professional cruisaders, one could mistakenly assume that the trip was somehow connected to religious fertility rites where the sacrifice of maidens has always played an important part. Should a cruise line ever worry about its occupancy rate, it certainly doesn't have to when it comes to maiden voyages as these are already booked out before the ship has even been built. But what makes people flock in droves onto a vessel that may still have teething troubles and not everything might as yet be running smoothly? Why does the common cruisader tolerate possible shortcomings when he pays top price? He simply wants to be there. And be there first. He may even immortalise the achievement by carving "Buster was here" into the railing.

There are many rungs on a cruisader's nobility ladder. First there is the humble crossing the equator baptism where being rubbed with fish waste has been abandoned in favour of being decorated with exotic paints. The next rung is the Atlantic crossing (also see Atlantic Crossing) or even a round-the-world-trip followed by the medal for "1,000 uninterrupted days on board". But all that is nothing compared to being on a maiden voyage, which can only be surpassed by having been on SEVERAL maiden voyages. You easily recognise one such ennobled individual because he no longer walks across the deck, he glides. He also quietly listens to the rest of the guests comparing their experiences on various other ocean liners and nods benignly until playing his trump card at the very last moment: "Three maiden voyages!" The rest of the round is instantly awestruck. They are looking at the reincarnation of Captain Ahab, at Christopher Columbus' and Sir Francis Drake's successor and no longer need to worry. Should the need arise, that sun of a gun will drag the ship away from the storm with his bare teeth, seal that nasty leak after the collision with the iceberg with two towels (also see Towels) and a lot of chewing gum and always know where there's an unoccupied deckchair. From then on the maiden voyage expert won't ever have to put his hand in his pocket again – others will do that for him. Here's some advice: to exploit the current cruise craze you can always conjure up some fictitious names of ships on which you allegedly made your maiden voyage. Do, however, remember to refer to the *Ivan the Terrible* as 'she'!.

# MAN OVERBOARD

To this day the women's emancipation movement has been unable to enforce gender equality by replacing the distress call with "woman overboard". But ever since a prominent German feminist apparently once said: "No woman is dumb enough to fall off a ship," the issue was laid to rest. To be politically correct, the crew, during their emergency training, are taught to use the term "person overboard" although this contains an additional syllable and is more time-consuming should its use be necessary.

In an emergency this call is vital to offer the one who fell overboard a fair chance of survival. For the officers on the bridge it is the cue to launch the fast rescue boat (a particularly fast boat, as the name implies), to quickly change course of the mother ship (a term the feminists DO agree with) regardless of the rapidly sliding glasses and guests, and execute a U-turn to save the lost passenger. As one can imagine, this manoeuvre may take a minute or two considering the size of an average cruise liner. The next challenge is to spot a relatively small head in the vast ocean. Therefore every passenger who sees another involuntarily leaving the ship should throw whatever comes to hand into the water, whereby lifebelts have first priority. Everything else should also be able to float. It's not much use to bombard the unfortunate individual with bottles and glasses as the objects thrown after him are intended to facilitate his location. Official bodies also recommend tossing deckchairs over board. These are the instructions from the powers that be. But entre nous: who in their right mind would hit on the idea of tossing one or more precious deckchairs into the sea? Where would you place your towel (also see Towels)? Besides, one less passenger renders the battle for the coveted deckchairs considerably more easy. You should therefore think carefully if the life of a rival guest is worth the loss of a precious deckchair. Should you have been previously acquainted with the struggling passenger, you could always fling some tables and chairs after him. As an old cruisader saying goes: better to eat while standing than to stand while tanning.

# MARITAL CRISIS

A cruise is a wonderful, wonderful thing. But as wonderful as it may be, it is usually quite long as well. And after a while, let's say from about day ten on, you'll sooner or later witness a substantial domestic quarrel. Three basic ingredients mainly act as the catalyst: 1. an inside cabin, 2. a prolonged stretch at sea, 3. bad weather. While the first few days are spend in peaceful harmony and most men still want to fulfil her every wish (especially inside their inside cabin), their attentive behaviour noticeably deteriorates at the latest a week into the voyage. The issue of shoes may serve as a vivid example. At the start of the trip the man still chuckles with amusement at the bizarre amount of footwear completely covering the carpet. But from day four he starts growling as he repeatedly trips over her stilettos. From day six the occasional dainty sandal finds itself being kicked around the cabin and from day eight the first pair of espadrilles is being flung across the (inside) cabin. This is it. Nerves are stretched to the limit and the imminent major row starts gathering momentum.

It is particularly satisfying for the fellow voyagers when these marital conflicts make it as far as the public areas. Even *Big Brother* doesn't afford as much insight into other people's most intimate details. An estimate 1200 guests, for instance, were once privy to a lady approaching retirement age bitterly berating her husband at the on-board theatre a few minutes before the performance started. The man was already seated some rows apart from where his better half was standing and initially she simply wanted to impart the message that she was going to powder her nose and would he keep a seat for her. Due to the relatively loud background music and gender specific communication problems the message apparently didn't reach the receiver. The lady worked herself up into such a rage that the rest of the theatre goers became quite scared. They did, however, also form an extremely clear impression of whatever the woman disliked about her spouse and what she generally thought of him before she made her exit in a fury, never to be seen again.

Some guest relations managers, who personally have a rather sceptical view of matrimony or marriage-like alliances, occasionally toy with the idea of inviting people like the above mentioned lady as a speaker on honeymoon cruises. Somebody like her should certainly manage to transport one or the other of those rose-tinted spectacle wearers from cloud nine down to cloud eight.

# MEDITERRANEAN

In the summer months the Mediterranean is without doubt the favourite destination of the international cruise industry. Hardly any other region satisfies as many different interests and offers an abundance of incredible sights in such a small area: Spain, Italy and France via the North African coastal countries of Morocco, Tunisia and Egypt right up to Israel or the Lebanon. This means cultural legacies from the old Greeks to the ancient Romans, from Carthage to the pyramids, from Moses to the crusades. For us Central Europeans a Mediterranean cruise also has the added benefit of accessibility, which makes getting to the ship relatively inexpensive, at least when compared with a plane ticket to the Caribbean.

   The affordability of a Mediterranean cruise naturally also appeals to the less affluent, i.e. younger people. Suddenly a mini break on a cruise ship presents a desirable alternative to a week of relentless partying on Ibiza. This is where two opposing interest groups collide. The younger generation wants to party; ideally right around the clock. Of course, every cruise ship is equipped to cater for those needs, although not in all their extreme forms. Young people celebrating special occasions like the ever popular stag parties soon miss the buckets and the XXL straws to slurp their Sangria, but usually quickly find alternative means to imbibe vast quantities of alcohol. Before long the jolly party goers will have reached a level of inebriation that frequently results in the loss of the command of their mother tongue which won't be regained for days even after immediate booze withdrawal. But at this stage sudden abstinence is linked to physical discomfort, so what can the party enthusiast do? He must maintain his level of intoxication, at all costs. Or, more accurately, at the cost of the more mature voyagers' comfort.

But should the cultured traveller let his well-earned holiday be wrecked by a handful of legless, obnoxious idiots? Certainly not! Don't bother complaining, which would inevitably lay the foundation for your next stomach ulcer; affect indifference instead. Always bear in mind: they're only having fun. When you're pelted with ice-cubes – they're only having fun. When your better half's bikini top is forcefully being removed – they're only having fun. When you find yet another repeat performance of Bang, Bang, Rosie hard to endure – they're only having fun. When the next round of vodka and Red Bull ends up on your deckchair instead of making it to the lads – they're only having fun. You can also exploit their fun addiction for your own ends. Stand the jaunty gentlemen a round of drinks and show them the biggest attraction on board: the diving platform on Deck 8. Promise them further refreshments for the best acrobatic dive and wait. Once the last member of the gang has plunged into the sea after a wobbly somersault, you should be kind enough to point him in the direction of Mallorca. Humming the exquisite lyrics to Bang, Bang, Rosie, you'll soon sink back into your deckchair, totally relaxed and say to your partner: "they were only having fun!"

# MESS

Many an observant passenger will have wondered why the crew appears to have such a penchant for the untidy or problematic because when guests should happen to overhear their private conversations they can't fail to notice the frequent mention of their having just come from the mess, being on their way to the mess or about to meet at the mess. This is particularly surprising since cruise ships are renowned for being highly organised and spotless (the term shipshape comes to mind). Here we are dealing with a simple misunderstanding. The mess on a ship is the room where the crew is fed. It is similar to the dining facilities in a youth hostel and often also to the prevailing atmosphere therein where the many nationalities are reflected by the proverbial Babel of tongues. Different culinary preferences are catered for and thus Asian cuisine is often available alongside international dishes.

Ship's officers have always enjoyed special privileges aboard. This also applies when it comes to food. They dine in the officers' mess where they're served the same fare as their underlings, but can devote themselves to nautical problems without being unduly disturbed. Privileged as they may be, in contrast to the lucky guests, and much to their regret, they aren't being served wine with their meals as many cruise lines don't allow their staff to drink or at least limit their intake of alcoholic beverages.

# MUSIC

There are two things one can't escape from on a cruise ship: the ocean and music. When you're fighting a losing battle against seasickness in the loo – there's background music. When you wake up in one of the lifeboats at night and struggle to find your cabin – there's background music. And even when you question the huge bill for extras on your last day and are about to get all worked up about the fact that you never visited the on-board hairstylist – there's background music. But it's harmless, pleasant to the ear and entirely safe. As opposed to a certain song which is played when your beloved ocean giant leaves the mainland. This song has been specially selected or even composed for each cruise ship and becomes deeply anchored in the cruisader's mind over the course of his travels. Because it is not only played the first time the ship puts out to sea, but every time it leaves a port while the romantically inclined guest stands at the railing once again, sipping his cocktail. He acknowledges it with a gentle smile and misses it terribly should it be slightly late. The music has already ingrained itself in his subconscious.

Back at home it serves the same purpose as the bell did for Pawlow's dog, that poor creature the Russian scientist always fed while ringing a bell to prove that the animal's salivation was triggered by the sound. This is called conditioning. When the returned cruisader now hears "his" cruise song, let it be at a shopping centre, he displays the same conditioning symptoms as the dog. He begins to salivate in anticipation of the first cocktail, he gazes into the distance and involuntarily puts his arm around the lady beside him on the escalator, the rattling of which suddenly sounds like the rattling of the windlasses pulling in the hawsers. He can already smell the delicious evening meal and looks forward to the night's entertainment "Dreams of the Caribbean". Only when distracted by the resounding slap from the lady beside him, when he misses the last step, trips and falls flat on his face, does he awaken from his dream. But instead of pulling himself together and attending to his daily tasks, he automatically visits the nearest travel agent's where he books the next cruise on "his" ship.

Cruisaders already acquainted with this book can be recognised by their ear plugs with which they attempt to prevent the danger of conditioning. Just ignore them, those tight-fisted killjoys! If they can't afford another cruise, they shouldn't bother to embark on the first one.

# MUSTER STATION

The appearance of the full complement of guests on their muster station is the prerequisite for a successful sea rescue drill (also see Sea Rescue Drill). In an emergency the guests assemble at the muster station where they are bundled into the lifeboats. To prevent hundreds of cruisaders from capsizing a single rescue vessel, the ship has more than one muster station and as such also more than one lifeboat. (There are actually a lot more lifeboat places than passengers, but that's a well-guarded secret.)

But how do you find the station allocated to you? It's easy. They are arranged in alphabetical order. Your letter is displayed on the inside of your cabin and the outside of your lifejacket. On boarding a cruise ship most guests miss the ubiquitous green squares with arrows and letters. They lead, as one would imagine, to the various muster stations. Simple. So simple. And after the regrettable incident on the *Titanic*, the system is continuously being perfected. Despite all that, finding their station seems to present an insurmountable obstacle to many German passengers. This may be caused by linguistic confusion as the German word "Muster" means pattern. Thus on cruises offering various handicraft and needlework courses some knitting-obsessed Teutonic ladies eagerly look forward to the generous selection of patterns available on this specifically dedicated station. Easily confused are also English speaking passengers travelling with peacocks because everyone knows that the collective noun for peacocks is a muster.

For logical reasons all those assigned to a particular muster station with the same letter are also housed in the same part of the ship. If your cabin neighbours' noisy lovemaking has irritated you ever since you moved into your own accommodation, you can amuse yourself by trying to identify the culprits during those boring rescue drills on the basis of the letter on their lifejackets and their cabin number. After that it's up to you if and how you want to address those two.

## NAUTICAL QUESTION TIME

Some cruise ships host a question and answer session
with the Captain at some point during the journey (also
see Captain). If this goes ahead or not is, of course, up

to HIM. Whenever he decides that it does, the majority of the passengers will attend the event. Questions posed to the Big Cheese can be okay, embarrassing, and at times so bad that one is ashamed to belong to the human race, which is allegedly at the top of the evolutionary ladder.

Standard questions are:

- "How does one become a captain?"
- "How much fuel does the ship consume per day?"
- "Up to what gale force can we still sail?"

and

- "How high can the waves be before the carpet in the cabin gets wet?"

More often than not a child will enquire how much a Captain earns? This does, however, give rise to the suspicion that the kid only asked after being urged by his single mum and is usually the first highlight. The following is the sort of question that initially bores you and then makes you blush on behalf of the enquirer: "When the clamp on split half coupling mates with the gearbox output coupling to connect the boat propeller shaft to the gearbox, how is the shaft coupling secured to the propeller shaft?" ???????? is the mental reaction of most Captains to that. Tons of amateur nautical experts can't wait for the occasion to shine with their confused smattering of knowledge. This generally doesn't work out because the self-proclaimed expert's exaggerated self-importance becomes the focus of the audience and overshadows the question itself. There are, however, quite sensible questions as well. A logical-minded, 14 year old girl, for example, wanted to know: what actually happens to the ships when nobody wants to go on cruises anymore?

# NAVIGATION

Landlubbers are lucky creatures. As opposed to seafarers, they can be entertained by a pleasant voice on
lengthy car journeys: "Follow the road for 196 miles!"
or "Take the eighth exit at the roundabout!" or "Please
turn, if possible!" or "Turn, you nitwit!"

It's totally different on a cruise. The officers on the
bridge are very lonely people because up there they
don't have a cheerful voice telling them: "Follow the
ocean for 4,200 nautical miles!" or "Turn left after the
second reef!" or "Please dive, if possible!" or any other
similarly helpful advice. This particularly applies to the
officers on duty who are left with nothing but the sea,
the ship and themselves. It doesn't get much lonelier
than that. But on a busy or navigationally challenging
stretch all the decision makers assemble on the bridge,
deeply focussed, and monitor depth, height, width,
speed, traffic and much more. Therefore the bridge
looks like any dedicated sci-fi fan's ultimate spaceship.
Wall to wall high tech: radar, sonar, solar, minibar.
Monitors everywhere that inform the navigator about
things like another vessel on the same course moving
forwards, backwards or not at all. Or if that bright
dot is a carelessly discarded oil barrel or a surfacing
submarine.

The navigator shouldn't actually have to navigate
anymore. All the navigating is done by a computer.
Whenever the Captain embarks on a certain route for
the first time, he simply presses the "Remember!" but-

ton. The computer kindly obliges and one could theoretically let it take over whenever the route is repeated. But then it's like using a sat nav where the friendly voice keeps telling you to turn on a motorway or drive into the next road block. For that reason the officer on duty always has to keep an eye on his electronic colleague and the pleasant lady we know from our car has no place on the bridge.

## OFFICERS

A cruise ship's staff includes officers in charge of various departments. First among them are the officers of
the watch who basically live on the bridge and are in

charge of navigation. Then there are the safety officers whose title doesn't need an explanation. Furthermore there are engineering officers responsible for the smooth running of all the mechanical and electronic on-board equipment, including communication devices like the internet and phones.

In the public areas you'll find officers concerned with entertainment and the guests' general wellbeing. And that's only some of them. Knowing which department an officer represents is not always immediately apparent to the layperson. Officers' uniforms being of different colours, depending on the department they belong to, facilitates recognition. But should the cruise line not have specified such a differentiation in order to make it more difficult for the guest, said guest will have to revert to inspecting the colour of the officer's stripes and his emblem. The guest should then be able to decide if he should quiz the officer about the on-board entertainment or the diesel generators' current performance.

The officers' uniforms can inspire awe in the common passenger who considers them to be the authority to address with his enquiries or complaints. They thus find themselves having to deal with queries such as "Are there extra blankets to keep warm for passengers in outside cabins?" and "What time is the midnight buffet?" As far as complaints are concerned, officers may have to face accusations like there having been too much sand on the beach (after a passenger's shore excursion), the weather being not as warm as expected in Alaska (this passenger demanded a refund on those grounds), the engines being too noisy (the captain refused to turn them off), right down to the woman complaining that her lifejacket didn't match the colour of her shoes. All those enquires and complaints are actually true.

.

# ON-BOARD ANNOUNCEMENTS

On-board announcements, as the name suggests, are announcements made on-board. Today's cruise ships have loudspeakers installed in every conceivable nook and cranny, not least for security purposes. One does, after all, want to know when it is time to leave the ship in a life jacket, even when busy on the loo.

The possibility of communicating with virtually all the passengers at the same time does, however, also kindle an overindulgence in the facility. Not only the Captain uses the equipment for his daily announcements, but numerous other departments also misuse it to inform the passengers of more or less important details regarding the daily routine, right down to the restaurants' feeding times, especially and mainly on American mega cruise ships. Considering the size of these vessels, groups of hungry voyagers have to be divided into colours. The green group, for instance, is invited to dine from 6 p.m. onwards, the yellow group from 7 p.m. and the red group from 8 p.m., and woe to those who feel peckish outside their scheduled times. It gets exciting when two American liners with similar colour groupings are anchored side by side and those announcements can be heard on both ships. When all the yellows or reds storm the restaurants where the greens are already tucking into their starters. Now it gets interesting. As far as food is concerned and inside the restaurant (also see Restaurants) the common crusader doesn't tolerate any messing about.

The nightly entertainment is also announced over the speaker system. These notifications don't only sound as if read from a prompt, they are. Yet even this does not guarantee a flawless delivery as shall be illustrated by the following slip of the tongue during a nightly cinema announcement: "At eight o'clock we shall be showing *The Poseidon Adventure*. Get ready to pass the cockporn." Freud would have loved that one.

Listening is an absolute must when it comes to the shopping news. On some vessels you'll be thus acquainted with special promotions and the latest bargains. When one of the passengers with a familiar surname is paged shortly after, you could almost believe you're inside your local supermarket, eagerly awaiting the special offers for two pounds of mince or frozen pizzas and the opening of till No. 2. But it's not just the contents that renders a "message" com- or incomprehensible; the technical implementation frequently poses a major obstacle as well. Some announcers apparently stand a heartfelt 30 feet away from the microphone; others have evidently shoved it right down their oesophagus. With the first of these it then sounds like a bunch of schoolgirls whispering inside the gym and with the second lot like the final Klingon warning before blowing up the spaceship. Be that as it may: always listen carefully! Or you could just miss the announcement of all announcements which back in the day always included "… women and children first".

# ORIENTATION

The average cruise ship is big – very big. So big that one can easily get lost. Especially below deck where there are no optical aids such as the funnels. A lot of guests take an involuntary after dinner stroll on their way from the restaurant to their cabin when they promptly walk in the wrong direction after exiting the lift. By the end of their last day they've usually managed to find a point of reference which saves them from further inadvertent detours during their remaining 12 hours on board.

All this shouldn't unnecessarily bother the ship designers as occupied guests are happy guests. But when they can't even find their own cabins, they may also not find areas they definitely should such as the shops or the casino. Thus it was decided to assist the passengers with visual reminders. Each deck has wall charts on the stairwell displaying various views of the ship, some showing an aerial view of the deck, others a cross-section of the ship, additionally marked with the famous red dot "You are HERE". These charts are very handy if one can correctly interpret them. Many guests first stare at them in bewilderment, then acknowledge them with a knowing "Aha" before instantly taking the wrong direction. It's always fascinating to observe especially older married couples reminding each other of their shared experiences over years of being wed. The interested listener may thus overhear: "You couldn't even find the hospital when I was pregnant with our

Sharon." Rarely are those comments, which inevitably reopen old wounds, simply accepted by the accused, who more often than not counters with: "That's rich, coming from you of all people! You only ever tell me to go right or left when we're way past the turnoff." Such exchanges generally escalate into a debate about the point and purpose of a marital union in one's dotage and often end with a joint appearance before the purser (also see Purser) with the request for two single cabins.

It doesn't have to be like that. Because, as already mentioned, a cruise ship is big – very big. And everywhere are unexpected surprises waiting to be discovered. Go with the flow! Not every guest enjoys the privilege of accidentally ending up in the Captain's quarters. Don't plan; let your trip be an adventure! Enjoy the walk without reaching your intended destination, the wonderful experiences on your march to things afar. You never know what's around the corner, which is a bit like Gulliver's Travels without the unpleasant aspects. And when you really want to get back to your cabin in the evening, take the lift to your deck and take the wrong direction first, which also provides you with some exercise. As Mahatma Gandhi so wisely said: "The path is the goal."

# P

## PIRATES

Way before the crusaders, even way before the knights in search of the Holy Grail, emerged the first groups of sailors with a heightened need to acquire other people's stuff: the first pirates. These gentlemen had fallen through the then still rather loose-knit fabric of acceptable society and earned their living by redirecting cargo and even entire ships into their own home ports. The understandable resistance of those parted from their possessions frequently resulted in the loss of body parts so that the wooden leg, the eye patch and the hand-replacement hook became the buccaneers' trade mark. Over time, the profession, like so many others, created a corporate identity, i.e. a brand logo, and thus the "Jolly Roger" came into being, the black flag featuring skull and crossbones. Later complaints of plagiarism by the International Association of Independent Gravediggers (I.A.I.G.) were summarily dismissed.

While just a paltry 400 years earlier the exclamation "Pirates!" had been synonymous with death, devastation and depredation, the pirates' image gradually changed to that of a bunch of jaunty, hard-drinking fellows at an eternal, nautical stag party whose outfits also made excellent costumes on fancy dress occasions. Their symbols became cool, their deeds were trivialised and soon the fashion industry, too, recognised the skull and crossbones' allure. Once Johnny Depp had captured the Black Pearl as Captain Jack Sparrow, millions of ladies longed to share the ship's fate. Pirate parties with pirate cocktails were all the rage and the kids (also see Kids) and their minders performed pirate spectacles.

The attitude towards piracy was boisterous and silly until international fishing corporations, first and foremost the EU trawlers, hit on the lucrative idea of thoroughly depleting the fishing grounds at the Horn of Africa, off the coast of Somalia, for example. And now the local fishermen with their small boats found themselves in a similar situation to that of their colleagues a few hundred years before. When they attacked the first trawlers, the stance towards pirates abruptly changed also on cruise liners. On many ships the word could only be whispered or was replaced by freebooter. Still, pure terror reigned among the guests. As soon as any small boat was sighted swiftly approaching the cruise ship, it was only with extreme effort that the crew could prevent outbreaks of mass hysteria. And the guests' desperate bombardment of the small boat with champagne bottles and pineapples didn't stop until the captain's liberating announcement that 1. the probability of a pirate attack in the Baltic was small to non-existent and 2. the small vessel carried the summoned ship pilot. This relieved most of the guests, but was a bitter disappointment for the ladies who had hoped for an encounter with Captain Sparrow until the very last moment.

# POOL PARTY

All cats are grey in the dark and the sea is dead black apart from some shimmering lights dotting the ocean. This means one of the famous and notorious pool parties is in full swing on the lido deck of a cruise liner. Dancing the night away beneath the starry firmament at a pleasant temperature whilst swilling tropical drinks must be as close to paradise as it gets. These pool parties often have a theme, be it "The Night of the Pirates" or "The Gay 80s". And those two have more in common than one thinks.

The fear of piracy on international waters is growing and ships are installing ever new defence measures from electric fences to water cannons. But none of this is necessary on a cruise liner because of the 80s-themed pool party. Imagine you are a pirate approaching a cruise ship promising rich pickings under the cover of darkness. Your diesel-powered speedboat is quietly chugging along and nobody has as yet noticed you – apparently. But then your ears are assaulted by hundreds of voices roaring "Ole, Ole, Ole" at a volume that chills even you, the bloodthirsty pirate, to your very bones and quickly convinces you not to take on such a horde of lunatics.

On that note: To prevent a possible pirate attack, do your bit and enthusiastically throw yourself into the proceedings and join a thousand others in the ever popular conga line. Waking up in the drained pool, you will experience the sublime feeling of having contributed towards the safety on board.

# PORTSIDE

Some passengers blessed with a vivid imagination but sadly lacking in education believe the portside of a cruise ship to be the place where port is served after dinner. Their ignorance may be forgiven as another group of similarly deluded guests think the nautical term portside or port derives from the tradition of passing the port to the left during a meal. Not so. Nevertheless, and for entirely different reasons, portside is left. Right?

**The layman frequently finds it difficult to distinguish between port and starboard, but it's really quite simple:**

The average, right-handed sailor in the days of yore operated the rudder with his right hand and thus sat on the left (portside) facing forward towards the bow, prow or stem instead of the aft or stern which may also have been positioned windward or leeward (also see Windward & Leeward) depending on the direction of the wind. Starboard, however, i.e. the right, derives from the Old Norse "stýri" (steering) and "borð" (board) since the Vikings were also mainly right-handed and operated their steering oars from the right hand side of their longboats. These fearsome warriors called the opposite side "larboard" (where the cargo was loaded). Of course, this sounded much like starboard. As vessels were mainly moored on the left side at ports so the steering oar didn't get damaged, the term port was used instead to avoid confusion. This proved to be particularly helpful during naval battles where hard-of-hearing officers or those neglecting their auricular hygiene could easily mishear their admiral's orders at vital moments - with disastrous consequences.

A passenger merely has to remember these simple facts during a guided tour of his cruise ship so he will know its left and right, though he may find it difficult to concentrate on the tour guide's explanations at the same time.

An easier way to trigger the memory may be to bear in mind that the words port and left both consist of four letters. But if all that still hasn't sunk in and you don't want to seem ignorant in front of your baffled fellow passengers in need of enlightenment, just inform them that port is opposite to starboard.

# PURSER

The purser is one of the most important crew members. Repeat travellers know him as the chief in charge of the steward(esse)s and easily recognise him by the three and a half stripes on his shoulders. His name derives from the word "purse" and thus we know about his main area of responsibility. Paymaster, the other term occasionally used for the position, underlines this even more so. He handles all financial transactions on board apart from paying the crew whose members receive their salaries directly from the powers that be ashore.

Nowadays the biggest and most important source of income on a cruise ship are the passengers and the purser is mainly concerned with billing them. Guests usually also reserve their cabin when booking. Should anything be amiss regarding those, this also falls under the purser's remit. Which also illustrates why he is one of the most powerful people on board. If you ever find yourself in the precarious position of not knowing the lady who shares your inside cabin anymore and whom you can't stand although you're married to her, you're at the purser's mercy when you beg him to be relocated so you can finally have a holiday – away from her.

## QUALITY

A cruise's quality is greatly in the eye of the beholder. Should that eye be clouded by emotional disturbances such as love or frustration, an objective assessment is very much out of the question. The quality of a voyage can essentially be assessed from the point of its hardware and software; the hardware being the ship itself. The international cruise industry offers an extensive variety: from luxury liners with indoor oceans to hastily and economically converted cargo ships where the cabins still very much resemble their original purpose.

Then there is the food. On some ships you may have to skip five of the twelve daily meals if you still want to be fit for the nine-course midnight feast. On the less exclusive liners, although bread and water are inclusive, you can occasionally order delicacies such as the good old bacon butty or the Glaswegian favourite chicken tikka masala at the paltry price of £11.99 - simple fare sadly missed by luxury cruise ship passengers about six weeks into their journey.

The hardware also includes active and passive entertainment. While the more sophisticated liners boast skating rinks and surf simulators, the less sophisticated ones may still surprise by supplying deckchairs, even with optional cushions. And when on the former the evening's entertainment consists of one sensational show after the next, the latter features the guest relations manager who fancies himself as the ONLY true Karaoke star and doesn't take kindly to somebody else taking the microphone.

And this brings us to the software. Here we also differentiate: between employees and volunteers. The crew has already been discussed in a previous chapter and here, too, the quality varies from ship to ship. But they all certainly give their best, although even that may not always be enough. If on one type of ship you may get the impression that somebody from housekeeping is conveniently located in the closet beside your cabin or you feel like royalty with underlings constantly reading your every wish from your lips; on the other the staff may be so not bothered that you won't dare bother them either.

This leaves us with the volunteers, i.e. the guests. Nothing bonds voyagers more than communal bickering, preferably about quality. On luxurious liners passengers are frequently convinced that this has "badly deteriorated" and on the more humble kind the passengers have mostly "had better times" before. But in many cases judging the quality is determined by the emotional state of the above mentioned beholder. The professional moaner can easily perceive a luxury liner as the tackiest booze cruiser, just like the newly in love has the best time of his life on the latter. So, fall in love, and the quality of the ship will definitely be of secondary importance.

# R

## RECEPTION

The Mecca for those in need of advice, the Lourdes for those in search of direction, the ultimate place of pilgrimage for the dissatisfied on every cruise ship is the reception desk. The questions being asked and the complaints being aired here must be quite hard to digest in a sober state. Contrary to a hotel, guests don't check in at the reception, but usually at the terminal (also see Check-in). Therefore the reception is visited for just three reasons:

1. Queries
2. Payment for additional services at the end of the voyage
3. Complaints

As you can see, two of the three occasions are of a negative character. And in the case of the first it can indeed happen that the receptionist, no matter how obliging, is quite simply overtaxed by the query. This is confirmed by some of the passengers' more bizarre enquiries:

- Why are there no land excursions when we're at sea?
- Why does the ship not have cable TV?
- Does the crew also sleep on board?
- How do I recognise the snapshot the photographer took of me when my cabin number isn't marked on the back of it?
- Does the crew eat the guests' leftovers?
- Why isn't the ship being evacuated before the rescue drill?

Receptionists on a cruise liner must be extraordinarily well-balanced individuals who can conjure up an answer to any question, no matter how obscure. Apart from staying calm at all times, the receptionist must also be in command of his or her emotions as every complaint has to be recorded, effectively as proof of the seriousness of the concern. This log contains enough material for several sitcoms. Here are some examples:

An indignant elderly lady complained that the micro-wave in her cabin didn't work because her tea wasn't even nearly hot enough. Once it was explained to her that the supposed microwave was actually a safe, she still wasn't quite convinced and enquired about the purpose of the alleged timer to select the number of minutes to heat up her brew. Another amusing anecdote was supplied by a gentleman in his prime, i.e. his mid-fifties, who complained at the top of his voice about the disrespectful allegation of him being untidy. Nobody, not even his wife, had apparently ever accused him of being slovenly and he was highly affronted by the insinuated flaw in his character. His statement was met by blank stares from the receptionists. The summoned supervisor, too, was baffled by the complaint. Only when the man was quizzed more closely was some light shed on the matter. When he explained that he had repeatedly found the note "Please clean room" on his desk, the staff enlightened him that this was the door hanger for the housekeeping personnel. The sign with "Do not disturb" on the other side. The door hangers were subsequently amended. Much to housekeeping's chagrin as this drastically reduced the number of guests who had dutifully followed the instruction without complaining.

# RESTAURANTS

Sea air makes you hungry. This seems to be even more pronounced aboard a cruise ship, at least as far as the guests are concerned. On most of the bigger ships these torturous hunger pangs are relieved in two ways. One can either frequent one of the ordinary restaurants with waitressing staff where one generally pays a surcharge, or satisfy one's appetite faster, more effectively and, most of all, in a less inhibited fashion at the buffet.

Social interaction at buffets has been the subject of many a study. Should you be lucky enough to belong to a generation that has never known the type of hunger experienced in war times, the guests' behaviour at the buffet will give you an idea of how ruthless the fight for survival must have been in those days. And in our case the battle already commences outside the restaurant's portals. As much as two hours before mealtimes the first guests "accidently" find themselves at its doors and presumably reason: "Well, seeing that we're here... – besides, Trudy has trouble with her hip..." Thus they skilfully secure their pole position and can take turns relieving their bladders or attending to any other pressing business as long as one of the party guards their spot. But an hour before the doors open, at the latest, guests can no longer afford to indulge in that luxury. Because then the starting lines fill up, everybody pushes mercilessly and not an inch of space is wasted. Ten minutes before admittance the ravenous crowd extents all the way to the lifts and one ever more clearly hears a noise which could at first be confused with the infamous iceberg scraping against the hull. But in the Caribbean??? No, the sound emanates from hundreds of scratching hands and shuffling feet which compels the shipping companies to replace the carpet outside the doors and renovate the doors themselves every three months. A minute before the guests are let in, the hungry mob gets ever more agitated and first death threats towards the catering staff can be heard amidst the general disgruntlement. By now the atmosphere has reached seething point, mayhem is about to erupt and inside the restaurant some of the waiters are already considering the deployment of heavy artillery.

And then the big moment arrives and the doors to paradise open. Now the mood changes and resembles that in the Okawango Delta when the first raindrops fall after nine months of drought. Some of the famished need a drink; others need to hunt for food. Lightning fast the mob gets off the starting blocks and sprints towards its targets in record times arousing suspicions of excessive doping. Trudy's hip is no longer an issue. It is rumoured that some guests work themselves into such a frenzy that they fall overboard at the end of the restaurant in their endeavour to be the first at the buffet.

Once they've made it, one can witness astounding piling techniques rivalling the trickiest juggling acts performed by the Chinese National Circus. Some guests get highly inventive and erect a cucumber slice fence around the edge of their plates to increase its load capacity. At the table very few can enjoy their meal in peace as their neighbours continuously inform them about all the other absolutely unmissable culinary treats on offer. The extent to which an average human stomach can stretch is remarkable and peak performances can be achieved with a little training. Talking about training: those still able to talk after their extensive feast should quiz the waiter about upcoming mealtimes as there is no tactic, technique and personal record that cannot be improved upon.

# ROUGH SEAS

Whenever the waters are calm, the guests will be on deck at sundown enjoying their cocktails, snuggling into their beloved standing beside them and living the dream of life at sea. But sooner or later the sea rebels and shows its other face.

Once the vessel starts swaying, the time for wearing tight-fitting, floor length gowns is over. Because now the ladies have to be able to walk properly so they can keep their balance without toppling over. Just like real sailors. Ladies who are caught in their evening attire when the going gets rough are a popular target to be filmed by their partners. The boredom of unfortunate friends viewing the subsequent screening at home is often relieved by comments such as: "There's someone in dire need of a pee." Rough seas are, however, ideal to hide the sudden onset of intoxication. Those who deviate by more than 5 feet from either side of the straight line between bar and toilet can easily blame their condition on the ship's movement. This transitional phase where the organ of equilibrium in the inner ear, although irritated, has not yet completely cracked up, is still perceived as funny by most voyagers. But all too soon one of the guests' fervent exclamation "God, do I feel sick!" ushers in Phase 2.

Observant passengers should have anticipated what awaited them from the magical distribution of sick bags in the corridors and stairwells, intended to prevent a complete overhaul of the floor coverings. Depending on the severity of the ocean's wrath, the general focus shifts from the bars and restaurants to the infirmary (several decks below) where seasickness pills are dispensed in generous quantities. This also shifts the vessel's centre of gravity and thus marginally stabilises it, neatly killing two birds with one stone. Some of the guests return to the nightly entertainment after discharging their medication and/ or the pills are starting to work – unless the sea gets even rougher.

If the ship is caught in a heavy storm despite all the meteorological early warning systems, the lucky guests who don't have to (involuntarily) feed the fishes are entertained by characters resembling those from Michael Jackson's famous *Thriller* video. Zombies with a greenish tint to their complexion who are forced to follow the swaying ship's choreography and would dearly love to get back into their coffins. Experienced waiters correctly gauge the sufferer's current state regarding his appetite and enquire with discreet courtesy: "May I serve the next course or shall I just throw it overboard to save you the hassle?"

By now most ocean liners are equipped with spoilsport gadgets mounted to the hull beneath the waterline: the stabilisers. They counteract any undesired movement and keep the ship stable. Most passengers welcome this feat of engineering, albeit at the cost of some people's malicious glee. Should all else fail and nothing alleviates your nausea, you should quickly eat a bar of dark chocolate and drink a lot of peppermint tea. Although this doesn't help at all, the next time you feel the urge to vomit, it will at least taste of "After Eight".

## SEA RESCUE DRILL

Seven short and one long blast from the ship's horn are the signal for a sea rescue drill. According to international maritime law this has to take place within 24 hours of the passengers embarking on the ship. The drill explains the way to the lifeboats to the guests and instructs them in the use of safety equipment, which presents a near insurmountable hurdle for some of them. The lifejacket serves as just one example where some guests only realise after much bafflement that the hole in the upper third of the garment is intended for their head to poke through. Others wear them in a way that would make them float face down in the water in an emergency. But the well-trained and patient staff assist even the most challenged into the bright orange vests. Soon after the guests are shown the way to the muster station, the assembly point to board the lifeboats. Here the possible future crew of each lifeboat is checked for its completeness before the safety officer's address in several languages (live, depending on his or her linguistic talents). The entire event, when everything is briefly explained in case the need should arise, takes roughly 25 minutes.

As far as the passengers' interests are concerned, they can be divided into several characteristic groups:

1. The nerd – The nerd has already repeatedly watched the relevant educational videos on YouTube and knows whole passages by heart. He has practised putting on the lifejacket in the confines of his wardrobe to be prepared for any eventuality. The nerd also attends the buffet in his lifejacket, just in case, which during the drill provides him with the advantage of being able to snack on the leftovers stuck to it which have

inadvertently ended up there due to his lack of mobility while eating.

2. The casual type – This gentleman has been inconvenienced by the blast from the ship's horn and basically just wants to know what the hullaballoo outside is all about. Fly undone and shirt unbuttoned, he scuffles over to the muster station where he promptly falls asleep again. The advantage of the species: he's not much in the way. The disadvantage: he sleeps through his cabin number being announced. This wastes precious time while the more attentive wait for the twat's appearance, either freezing (in the Baltic) or perspiring heavily (in the Caribbean).

3. The prankster – Initially the prankster royally entertains himself and others by perfecting the art of donning the lifejacket. Now he's just standing at the muster station, bored out of his wits. This is where the little whistle attached to his lifejacket to alert people if in trouble comes in handy. He quickly employs it to delight crew and guests alike with a merry musical rendition which other pranksters are only too eager to join. Back at home, the prankster is easily spotted by his persistent oral herpes and a mixed infection of hitherto unknown germs other pranksters have left on his whistle as a silent salute.

4. The Now-or-Never type – This type spots his true love amidst the crowd of people and instantly realises that the ship offers far too many hiding places for the one he adores. Therefore he takes action

right away. The lady who has conquered his heart, however, has just risen from her bed, faces him without make-up, wearing her less than flattering jogging suit, and can think of a lot better things to do than flirting with the now-or-never type. Fortunately, the "now" part of the drill is over at some stage and hereafter the lady in question seems set to veer towards the "never" response when it comes to this type's amorous advances.

5. The Pessimist – The pessimist is convinced that the whole exercise is a waste of time and would rather stay in his cabin watching the proceedings on his television where they will hopefully be caught by the live webcams until all he can see are the underwater images. Despite all his pessimism he is still prepared for any emergency by having a rolled-up towel at his disposal which he can place outside his cabin door to protect himself from possible flooding. Here's a tip: don't listen to him!

Despite all that, one should pay attention about what to do in an emergency. That's why our brain is equipped with two distinct hemispheres. And here's another tip: it gets very crowded during a sea rescue drill. Crowded enough that some people faint without there being an emergency. Should you be prone to claustrophobia, it is advisable to procure a sick bag and fill it with muesli from the breakfast buffet. If you then hold the bag close to you during the drill while looking miserable, you'll find yourself with lots of space around you.

# SHORE EXCURSIONS

All cruises worldwide offer more or less interesting shore excursions. To find the one most suited to one's personal taste it is advisable to make an appropriate booking way before embarking on the journey or to attend a presentation on board and subsequently come to a decision and book. The talk will also stress the importance of solely opting for outings with the ship's own tour guides. Only they can guarantee safety and punctuality. Organised trips have the advantage of arriving at the sights surrounding the port without any major detours. Everything is under control and one isn't – and this is of the utmost importance to the average cruisader – in danger of starving to death. Every detail has been taken care of.

But is there an ultimate excursion one simply can't afford to miss? No! Sometimes it's even attractive not to accompany all the others. It is quite an overwhelming feeling to be suddenly more or less alone on an ocean liner designed for more than 2000 passengers. One doesn't have to reserve the deckchairs or queue at the buffet. One can delight in the most popular massages at any time and even enjoy the sauna without any unpleasant physical contact. If you'd rather exchange this feeling for dusty old pyramids, an overcrowded Coliseum or the endless lines of tourist outside the Catherine Palace, so be it. It's your holiday. Your choice. But when you're leaning against the railing, nursing a cocktail after a truly relaxing day on board, and witness 2000 sweaty, exhausted sightseers emerging from their tour busses or the lone tourists ripped off of everything but their underwear frantically waving after the departing ship, you'll know that you made the right decision.

# SHUFFLEBOARD

Shuffleboard is one of the oldest games played on cruise ships. Even the ancient whalers played it with a grey whale's sternum pushing a dolphin's kneecap onto a number field. This is, of course, pure conjecture, but the fact remains that this game was already played on the *Titanic*, albeit not for very long. Another fact is that shuffleboard is as appealing as tomato juice is on a plane trip. The allure fades as soon as you get home. Nowadays shuffleboard is played by pushing a wooden or plastic disc, roughly the size of the puck used in ice hockey, with a cue over the scrubbed deck into a scoring area much like a kiddies' hopscotch grid. One therefore often sees cocktail inspired individuals late at night remembering their childhood by risking a total write-off of their ankle joint or a major hamstring injury when they merrily hop across the grid. The version with the cue is considerably less dangerous, unless the implement is used as a weapon – which isn't all that far-fetched among the more competitive types.

In the layman's premature opinion shuffleboard is an unemotional game for the older generation without being too physically taxing. Not so. The players suddenly develop unexpected ambition, emotions reach boiling point, fractions of an inch are hotly contested and the battle lines are drawn. And then the first of the contestants recalls the introductory kendo course at the adult education centre or simply that the cue can also serve as a cudgel. And those who still claim that the game is boring have never yet slurped a peace cocktail with their shuffleboard opponent on being released from the infirmary. Through a straw, of course, and with the less swollen side of the mouth.

# SLIMMING

The only thing to get increasingly slimmer will be every voyager's chance of achieving just that. Brutally put: losing weight on a cruise is next to impossible. To blame is the rich assortment of delicious food and drink of any imaginable kind, available more or less round the clock. How can anyone resist? At least that's the excuse of those neatly trying to hide the real reason behind their overindulgence. Admittedly, most of what's on offer in the restaurants (also see Restaurants) differs greatly from the microwave fare consumed in the average bachelor household. But what weighs even more heavily is the fact (and the guest later on) that the food is usually included in the package deal. It's been scientifically proven that a meal's attractiveness is substantially enhanced when it's free. The principle is roughly the same as that of a clearance sale: everything must go!

The clearance sale comparison can also be applied to some passengers. You will instantly recognise the seasoned food bargain hunter from the epic portions piled up on his plate. Here the rule of thumb is: the stingier the guest, the fuller the plate. But by Day 3 at the latest his guilty conscience pipes up on account of his biblical gluttony. And now the first slice of pineapple appears beside the estimated 4000 calories he intends to devour. Pineapple, the miracle fruit that can apparently pulverise all those calories. Or suddenly the new motto is low carb and, lo and behold, only a single little potato has strayed among those two schnitzels in cream sauce and the seven pork medallions. While the ladies remember the latest dieting advice the men approach the flab problem a lot more pragmatically – at the on-board fitness centre. Although they've only passively participated in any kind of sport for the past 35 years, they're now convinced they can transform five kilos of the finest body fat into tough muscle in one afternoon and address the fitness trainer with the words: "Are those all the weights you can muster up around here?" They will ask for additional ones and proceed to strain and push until their muscles and the trainer's eyes are stinging. Then our beefcakes wriggle into a tank top, don sandals with white socks and feel like Arnie after having secured the Mr Universe title even though they struggle to lift their fork at dinner. Such violent body-enhancing exercises frequently result in hospitalisation (also see Hospital) where the latest Chippendale recruit has to revive his circulation. And, ladies, if you now have to feed your loved one through a beaker because the 120 pound dumbbell smashed his gnashers during the triceps workout, forget about low-carb diets or food combining. Pamper him –he did it all for you, after all!

# SMOKING

Whenever you are looking for a particular place on board on your first few days and you can't find a crew member to direct you, ask a smoker. No other guest knows the ship as well as the tobacco addict. Because he has investigated where he can and cannot smoke within minutes of boarding and therefore knows the ship like the back of his hand. On some American cruise liners he would be hard pressed to find a spot where he can indulge in his habit as there's a smoking ban on the entire ship. This is, however, the exception.

Basically the same smoking rules apply on cruise ships as do in their country of origin and in no other country are they as strict as the United States of America. Of course, most European liners also have certain regulations. The good news: smoking is allowed. The bad news: not everywhere. Just in specified areas. And those are not only recognisable by the smell or the fumes rivalling those spouting from the funnels, but also by the noise level. Following a slight variation of the old saying "home is where the smoke is", the smoking areas are considerably crowded and a boisterous atmosphere prevails. Through the curtailment of one's liberties, the implied criminalisation and marginalisation, smoking suddenly acquires an aura of the disreputable, the forbidden, and therefore becomes attractive. One quickly feels transported back to one's youth: the first secret cigarette, the first beer and the first snog. And often the smoking areas are also frequented by people who gladly suffer the polluted air to be amidst cheerful company. For those who want to quit the habit, being on a cruise ship is the worst place for their efforts to be crowned with success (also see Slimming).

By the way, seafaring folk fear nothing more than fire. The costly experiment of smoking inside your cabin should suffice to convince you. Within seconds, the smoke alarm will be triggered and even sooner the entire fire brigade, complete with protective clothing, respirator and power hose, will be assembled outside your door. Do not say "Ooops" at that moment unless you would like to become more closely acquainted with the Captain. So, be careful and always discard your butts in one of the specially provided ashtrays, not the floor of the deck, and certainly do not nonchalantly fling them overboard. Should the butt be blown through an open balcony door into a cabin, and that cabin happens to be yours, you may have to wave goodnight to your first night of passion with your latest conquest. And that would be a shame.

# SOUVENIRS

Souvenirs are beautiful reminders of an even more beautiful time. As you so correctly guessed, the word comes from the French and means keepsake or memento. But souvenirs are not only intended as a memento for the purchaser but also bring joy to the loved ones back home. And who isn't overjoyed when he receives that unique 6 foot wooden giraffe, the tasteful ashtray featuring a Spanish bullfighter, an authentic beer stein, a comfortable camel saddle, that adorable polar bear made from rabbit fur or a real Caribbean straw hat that makes an excellent frisbee after being extracted from the bottom of the giver's suitcase.

All sorts of headgear or other items of clothing are generally among the most popular of souvenirs, first and foremost the T-shirt. This usually bears witness to the wearer's love of a particular place with the words "I ♥ …". After having been on a cruise with several destinations, this can quickly border on polygamy. But it fulfils its intended purpose of reminding the observer that the wearer has enviably been there. And then there is the kind of apparel the buyer considers to be eminently becoming and practical when worn at home (loincloth, kilt, toga) which serves his circle of friends and acquaintances as a memento that their owner has always been a bit soft in the head.

Cruisaders especially love objects with the ship's name, any kind of image of it or ones which even vaguely remind him of it. Towels (also see Towels) feature at the top of the list. But not the ones from the shop, but those from the cabin. The friendly housekeeping staff will, naturally, be delighted when they don't have to deal with so much dirty laundry on the last day. And, of course, the towel is included in the package deal and, of course, you will use it again on your next cruise. But the cruise lines don't view this in quite the same way. They'll turn a blind eye as far as the towels are concerned, but once the wall-mounted hair dryers disappear, the bed linen as well as the quilt, or even the TV (which fits so much more easily into the passenger's luggage in the age of flat screens), they get a tad annoyed. Which is why they ignored a former passenger who wanted to know why the dedicated cruise channel didn't work once he tried to watch it at home.

# STARBOARD

Opposite of port (also see Portside)

# STRIPES

The officers aboard a cruise ship are easily recognisable by their gold stripes. The more of them, the more important they are. These stripes, depending on the uniform, are either displayed on the jacket sleeves or on the epaulets of the jacket or shirt. The number of stripes varies from one (low-ranking officer) to four (Captain).

Contrary to popular belief, and with a bit of practice, zebras can also be distinguished by their stripes and thus the affinity to the animal kingdom is greater than generally thought.

At each of his appearances the captain (also see Captain) is hailed like a pop star. Naturally, nobody is antagonistic towards someone who holds their live in his hands. The common mouse will always be deferential towards the cat and the lion, too, is always addressed as Your Majesty. Given the opportunity, even the pig would rather be polite towards the butcher. Aboard a cruise ship one could nearly be led to believe that all the guests have made a pact to keep the captain in good spirits so he doesn't entertain any silly notions. But this is far from true. Hidden behind the admiration or even deification of the captain lies the inborn respect for stripes, particularly when they are gold or yellow. The above mentioned, common zebra also has stripes, but does that prevent the lion or the hyena from being nasty towards it? It doesn't. Because they are black (or white, depending on your preference). Yet a wasp or hornet with its yellow stripes inspires a healthy respect. Especially humans give them their maximum attention and everyone waves frantically even before the insect has departed again. Yellow stripes – Voilà!

What do we learn from this? Respect for a cruise ship Captain is not a voluntary or rational response but one we inherited from our ancestors. And that's the way it should be. A hearty slap on the back combined with the slightly clumsy attempt at fraternisation: "Hi, I'm Wally. And you are?" are usually met by the Captain's obstinate refusal to engage in first name terms. Don't ever forget: a captain can put you ashore at the next port if he believes you endanger the safety on board. And guests who are inclined to touch him, the nautical god, pose a not to be underestimated security risk.

# SUPERSTITIONS (SEAFARING)

Remembering that just a 100 years ago most sailors couldn't swim explains why they were extremely devout and pious – at least on board. The rough and wet reality of early seafaring life with the constant fear of capsizing, falling overboard or being devoured by sea monsters was, of course, an ideal breeding ground for all sorts of religious faiths – as well as superstition.

To this day cruise ships have no Deck 13 or cabins ending in the dreaded last digits 13. Superstition was, however, far more prevalent in the olden days. Sailors did, for instance, toss some coins into the ocean for luck. And lucky it proved to be. Mostly for the archaeologists who retrieved them centuries later. The mariners also nailed shark fins to the mast for strength and speed. It is rumoured that a passenger once nailed his left trainer to the funnel to achieve the same end: strength and speed. And, indeed, his voyage did come to a remarkably speedy end despite his extra strength.

Back in the old days the crew was also convinced that the souls of deceased seafarers reincarnated in marine birds like the seagull or the albatross. Today this means that whenever you see a seagull with four gold stripes circling the ship, you'll know that the captain has died. Cats on board are also meant to be lucky. Unlike women, who are supposedly unlucky. One can still find quite a few ladies on cruise ships who are aware of this and fear they may not be tolerated on board. For this reason the apparently start purring whenever an officer approaches them.

## TENDER

Tenders are the boats which ferry passengers to and from the cruise ship. "Wait a minute," exclaims the ambitious railway enthusiast, "aren't they the...?" Exactly. With the old steam locomotives the tender was the coal car right behind the engine. The same railway fan could now logically conclude that in the steamship era the coal to fire the engines was pulled behind the ship in a tender. But he would be wrong.

It hasn't been recorded who first coined the term tender because in other ship categories these accompanying vessels have different names. Sailing ships have dinghies, the rowing boats on commercial ships such as whalers are called gigs and daughter boats are fast support boats carried aboard a larger vessel. Tenders on cruise liners are used as lifeboats in an emergency and carry the guests ashore and back whenever the ship can't or doesn't want to enter a port. Apart from excursions during the voyage this can also be the case at the very start of the cruise when the ship, for whatever reason, isn't anchored at the port. Here it can happen that a guest's first ocean-going experience takes place on such a tender. Should the sea now also be quite rough (also see Rough Seas), the passenger will already feel seasick before the cruise has even started. Thus afflicted guests will board the mother ship with great reluctance and some cruise novices are rumoured to have abandoned their travel plans altogether or only embarked on their voyage after much persuasion.

The majority of passengers, though, love the whole tender experience and feel more closely connected to the ocean. They may not enjoy themselves as much in an emergency, however, because then this vessel doubling as a lifeboat has to be filled to capacity. Many tenders therefore have bum imprints painted on their benches so everybody knows where to sit and no space is wasted. These "bums" are roughly 15 inches apart – and there are American cruise liners. Enough said to expose yet another case of the discrepancy between planning and reality. Which may also explain why one passenger's suggestion to install beverage vending machines in the rescue boats was ignored. The cruise operators were presumably also scared of the potential headline: "Died of thirst through lack of change!"

# TOILETS

Toilets on cruise ships have a special and especially noisy characteristic. They slurp. And they slurp because they are vacuum toilets which use suction for the removal of its contents when you press the big button. For the ship these loos present not one but two advantages: they require far less water for flushing and their wastepipes have a considerably smaller diameter, which does, however, render the disposal of brought along small pets considerably more complicated.

The guests' reactions to this unfamiliar toilet technology veer between interest and fear. The interested type, mostly male, can spend hours in front of the loo pressing the big button over and over to delight in the wild vacuum. These enthusiasts may address their spouses thus: "Dumpling, how long do you reckon the toilet will take to suck up a whole role of loo paper, unwound, of course?" Insensitive wives generally react with: "Would you ever grow up!" But, to guarantee the harmonious continuation of the best time of the year, a wise partner should react with words like: "Wow, it's amazing what that loo can do. How clever of you to find out!" Should this partner now like a little more time to herself, to watch the latest episode of her favourite soap opera via satellite, the following reply would be useful: "Great – and now try to find out how long the toilet will take to suck up the  Sunday Times and supplements, in individual pages, of course."

The inquisitive passenger's desire to explore, however, is still far from satisfied. He now needs to find out if the toilet uses fresh or salt water. The more cautious will scoop up a sample with their toothbrush glass, which naturally distorts the taste. But the true scientist can be spotted by his wet fringe. And the elderly gentleman, who now munches his dinner without the aid of his dentures, has more than likely also flushed the toilet during the taste test. Remember: always hold on to your false teeth when checking the vacuum toilet's water!

Timid types believe all the rumours attached to these weird and wonderful appliances. But it really is only a rumour that a chubby lady hermetically sealed the toilet with her considerable bulk so that she got stuck to the seat after pressing the big button. While awaiting the plumber's arrival, her husband already entertained great hopes of a better future in view of the numerous beauties gracing the pool. Another rumour has it that a middle-aged gentleman set his lawyers loose on the cruise company after the completion of his voyage claiming that he could allegedly prove that his manhood, particularly the two dangly bits, had been impaired by the suction to such an extent that they now dangled approx. two inches lower. But all this is just hearsay. And for that reason gentlemen with inferiority issues shouldn't be too hopeful when it comes to increasing the length of their little friend

.

# TOWELS

Towels aboard a cruiser are more than just towels. They also double as status symbol, banner, means of identification and reservation, substitute blanket and above all as a popular souvenir (also see Souvenirs). For the cruise line they are first and foremost a headache. Staggering statistics regarding the loss of towels on cruise ships make one wonder that the basic price of a cruise is still below £1,000. But that's the company's problem.

Towels provided on the cruise are preferred to the extent that the common voyager even refrains from exhibiting his own although his fellow travellers thus miss the fact that he spent his last vacation in Florida, as would have been clearly indicated by the large size print. The ONLY towel of choice on board is the ship's own. Their favoured use may be motivated by the fact that it is common policy on virtually all ships that it will be exchanged for a fresh one at any time, which saves the trouble of having to wash it. The ship's own towels also come in handy when one has arranged to meet a newly befriended couple at the beach with the words: "You'll recognise us from the towels." And true enough, one soon spots a cheerful group with those unmistakable towels – then another and another. Thus one finally has the chance of getting to know the entire contingent of one's fellow voyagers.

Cruise towels are also abused in order to indulge in the frowned-upon habit of deckchair-reservation.

Here one can quickly observe a fascinating phenomenon. Seeing that all deckchairs are reserved with identical towels, nothing would be simpler than settling down on any of these and claiming that one placed the towel there oneself. Yet there somehow appears to be a reflex-like inhibition, originating in the animal kingdom's ancient marking behaviour, not to spread out on out towel that has previously been touched by another person.

The ship's towels are also employed as a heating source by individuals who pass the night on deck instead of their cabin for whatever reason. Be it that a domestic quarrel (also see Marital Crisis) has driven them to find shelter elsewhere, or be it that they were banned from the cabin after some such dispute, or be it that something is taking place in the cabin following said dispute which is already setting the stage for divorce proceedings. Whatever the case, the sleeper is glad to find comfort in something as familiar as the cruise ship towel.

# TRAFFIC

The international cruise market is booming. Over the past few years it reported increases of up to 20%. In 2016 1.8 million Germans alone sailed the oceans – roughly equivalent to that nation's proportion of non-swimmers or the population of Hamburg. This is obviously a positive development in terms of employment statistics and more than likely also for some ports. For others, particularly in Europe, however, this means a volume of visitors one could term a "critical mass".

The picturesque fishing village of Portofino, west of Genoa, may serve as an example. It is so idyllic that it is often employed as a backdrop for international film productions. The little village is situated in a bay and its small harbour is more than filled to capacity once ten fishing trawlers and three luxury cruisers anchor there. Spread around the harbour are colourful little houses nestled into the surrounding rocks. And moreover there are quaint cafes, cosy restaurants, friendly ice-cream parlours and cute little shops. This place, straight out of a picture book, offers everything for the affluent guest to feel at home.

Particularly during the summer season Portofino is a not to be missed destination for American cruise ships. On record days up to five ginormous ocean liners are anchored off its bay and unleash their passengers onto the romantic fishing village on tenders (also see Tender). The average tourist not only has to see Portofino, but also photograph or film it. And thus snapshots are created which are hard to surpass in their uniqueness:

"Romantic view of the ocean" - 30 tenders in various shades of orange in the foreground, predominantly white cruise ships in the background and in between a little bit of blue – the sea.

"View of the harbour from the ship" - 30 rivalling tenders in the foreground covered in the blue mist of their exhausts fumes and predominantly sunburnt tourists' bodies leaning against the pier.

"The quaint little café" - predominantly sunburnt bodies in the foreground and the upper left corner of the roof of the building housing the quaint little café.

"Picturesque architecture" – predominantly sunburnt tourists in the foreground with roofs and rocks featuring in the upper third of the image.

"Our ice-cream parlour" – mostly obscured by a smudge on the lens due to the kerfuffle; vague outlines of predominantly sunburnt people with and without ice-cream in the background.

A Tipp: Portofino is stunningly beautiful when not crawling with sightseers and off-season. For all those who can't wait, however, there are wonderful coffee-table books with incredible photographs: little in the foreground and a shockingly deserted village in the background.

# TYFON

The gigantic signal horn on a ship, including cruise ships, is called a typhon. It is located at the prow, generally above the bridge and, with the aid of compressed air, produces a loud, deep and ear-shattering sound which can be heard far across the sea as well as the neighbouring mainland. This air horn, originally intended for signalling, is actually only used when the ship casts off (also see Anchors Aweigh) as a farewell to the envious crowd assembled at the pier. The harbour master generally replies with a similar signal sound. Both sounds touch the ordinary cruisader's very soul and instantly convince him that he is, indeed, somebody special. Such a racket is, after all, usually only permitted on Guy Fawkes Night.

So the typhon is the ship's hooter or horn and its deployment varies greatly compared to that of a car horn which is far more frequently used – mostly illegally. The reasons are manifold and we shall therefore only explore a few of them:

1.  (To serve as a) Reminder – When a lady is being collected by a gentleman at a mutually agreed upon time to see a movie, the sporting motorist reminds the lady, who isn't already waiting for him on the pavement, to hurry up with two short honking sounds. On a cruise ship this practice is unknown as the ship rarely collects anyone to go to the cinema.

2. Admonition – In the case of a motorist inadvertently taking a wrong turn or shamelessly trying to park in a spot already previously earmarked by another, his astute rival enthusiastically honks his horn (several honks of medium length) to engage the traffic offender's attention before he can complete the offence. The honking sound is often accompanied by the upstanding citizen wildly gesticulating inside the car or by his spouse jumping out of the car. On a cruise ship parking spaces have been reserved well in advance and the captain rarely brings his better half along.

3. Punishment – Should a continental motorist, despite the presence of more vigilant road users, manage to complete a punishable act like overtaking another vehicle (whose driver has forgotten the exact location of the accelerator) from the right, he is instantly punished at the crime scene by a prolonged honk followed by several short ones. This is also accompanied by wild gesticulation. Again, this doesn't apply to a cruise ship as overtaking from the right is common practice on the world's oceans.

4. Easing traffic congestion – The biggest miracle which can be accomplished by targeted honking is the easing of traffic jams. As long as enough motorists take an active part, things will be considerably expedited: stalled vehicles start more quickly, accident victims miraculously recover, accident scenes basically clear themselves and even bottlenecks suddenly get more accommodating. It is therefore a mystery why this practice hasn't been adopted

by the shipping industry, for instance in cases of congestion on the Suez Canal.

And here's a tip: should the hairdryer in your cabin cease to work, wait until the ship leaves the port and head for the prow. The typhon's acoustic pressure will squeeze any moisture from your hair in seconds flat. This also helps when you're dissatisfied with the perm you acquired shortly before the cruise.

And here's another: The hospital, to address the damage to your eardrums, is usually found on the lower decks.

.

# UNDER THE WEATHER

See H for "Hospital".

# V

## VIDEO

The advantage of video cameras as compared to ordinary cameras is that they don't go "click". Otherwise one would quickly feel like being part of a Japanese group on their all-inclusive tour "Europe in Three Days". Although, or even because, video technology has already conquered Japan, it is not yet as prevalent there as it is on cruise ships where everything even remotely interesting is filmed. The sea rescue drill, the buffet, the cabin, the vacuum toilet, the theatre, arriving at, anchoring in or leaving the harbour. Mum at the bow, mum at the stern, mum being massaged, mum at sunset, mum happy and mum unhappy. The latter occurs when mum is being afflicted by the dreaded seasickness. While she's staring at the ceiling, pale as a ghost and utterly unable to move, she remembers the advertisements where everything looked so different.

And yet seasickness is not a sickness at all but simply an irritation of the inner ear, although beholding the sufferer one could easily classify him or her as being sick. Men are more sensitive to the torture they have to endure. In other words women have to endure their husbands' whingeing as well as their own misery. Despite all that it is often easier when the men are also sick, because when they aren't, they frequently become mischievous. On days when the hospital's corridors are already overflowing with seasick individuals and it looks like a scene from a disaster movie there's always a husbands who will, armed with his camera, try to produce a reality TV episode featuring his wife. The ambitious cinematographer is frequently only stopped in his tracks when he slips on the seasickness's end product and now needs hospital treatment himself.

## WEDDINGS

It is common knowledge that God scheduled the exchange of wedding vows to take place before the marital dispute. A fact many unmarried couples for some inexplicable reason choose to ignore. And if one intends to have a good row on a cruise ship one may as well get married on one. But it's not as simple as that. A Captain's powers are limited where romantic popular belief deems them to be omnipotent. He CAN NOT marry a couple, at least not in a manner that's legally binding in most countries. A wedding is a secular contract entailing the presence of a statutory representative. This means it's not valid without a registrar. With one exception: according to Maltese law a Captain can take on the role of registrar outside the twelve-mile-zone and perform weddings which are legal – in Malta. And one tour operator actually offers this service. But one still has to have the wedding registered in one's own country afterwards. Otherwise it is common practice for an official to come on board. Alternatively one can have the ceremony performed by the Captain, with a registrar in attendance, at a European port, all inclusive of an atmospheric ambience and an emotional after party. However, should you already be wed, you can get married again by the Captain on nearly all cruise liners and renew your vows in a truly romantic way. According to official surveys, most cruisaders find it a pity that the Captain is not authorised to perform valid marriage ceremonies. Unofficial surveys (particularly among occupants of inside cabins) showed that even more cruisaders regret that the Captain is not empowered to divorce anyone

# WINDWARD & LEEWARD

Most landlubbers only know windward and leeward, terms which are second nature to seafarers, from crossword clues. These nautical expressions, which are nearly always cited together like Batman and Robin or Beavis and Butthead, describe the sides of the ship either facing or facing away from the wind. Unlike portside (also see Portside) or starboard (also see Starboard), one doesn't necessarily have to remember those two terms, but knowing what they mean can prove exceedingly useful in many situations. Experienced crossword solvers are, of course, aware that leeward is the side facing away from the wind. If you stand on this side of the ship gazing at the ocean, the wind is on your back. Remembering this can considerably ease your stay on board.

Smokers who've flicked their butts overboard on the windward instead of the leeward side (which is not permitted, anyway) are easily recognisable by the black, worm-like stains on their T-shirts or the red, worm-like marks on their foreheads, similar to the Hindu symbol guarding against the evil eye (also see Smoking). Enamoured couples with matching hairdos, who are enjoying a to-die-for sunset during a strong breeze on the leeward side, will afterwards either sport identical flat patches at the back of their heads (short hair) or try to pull the hairs out of their mouths which the wind has blown between them while they were engrossed in a lengthy French kiss (long hair). And should you be one of those sensitive individuals suffering from the dreaded seasickness, you should, without fail, relieve yourself on the ship's leeside if you'd rather not be reunited with your lunch.

And yet standing on the windward side can have its advantages. This is related to the skin losing its elasticity due to the ageing process or the excessive intake of strong liquor on the previous night. If you notice in the morning that the amount and depth of your wrinkles would expose one of the above mentioned facts, simply park yourself on the windward side and let the breeze do its magic. But here, too, you shouldn't mix up windward and leeward if you want to avoid that the bald patch at the back of your head, although wrinkle-free, becomes all the more visible.

## X-RAY

When embarking on a cruise, not only is your person scanned with a metal detector for spontaneously brought along weapons or other frowned upon objects, your hand luggage and the souvenirs you acquired on shore excursions are also subject to safety checks. Everything is placed on a conveyer belt, similar to those at airports, and X-rayed.

The thoroughness with which this security check is conducted does, however, vary from destination to destination. There are countries where the scanner reacts noisily to possible illegal items, but nobody, including the security personnel, pays any attention. The scanner whistles, hoots and bleeps while the people in charge calmly discuss the last soccer match. The fifteen foot long original reproduction of the Sphinx glides majestically and unhindered along the conveyor belt, as does the authentic Samurai sword which has just severed a fly in half during its attempt to settle on somebody's suitcase. The SS-20 medium range missile, purchased in Cuba at a bargain price, or the good-as-new fuel rods, which had been on offer in St. Petersburg, are acknowledged by a short nod before you're waved on.

But not everything that doesn't bleep can simply be taken aboard. Most cruise ships have stringent hygiene regulations, particularly when it comes to foodstuffs. But here, too, security personnel in some countries aren't too fussy. They frequently let the ham from the Bodega or entire half pigs pass and aren't overly concerned about the colour-wise interesting kefir in whose fatty acids evolution is presently creating a brand new type of fungus.

But as soon as you place an innovative video camera on the belt, this astounding piece of technology is inspected, checked and tested. The exercise is, however, purely performed to satisfy the staff's personal interest and the device will soon (ca. 20 minutes later) be handed back to you with an appreciative smile. By the way, the same applies to coffee table books featuring Heidi Klum or Jennifer Love-Hewitt – just in case you are planning to smuggle something really illegal onto the ship.

## YACHTS

Many a passenger aboard a cruise ship will ask himself or the Captain: "What is the difference between a boat, a ship and a yacht? A smart Captain once replied: "You will find yourself on a boat when the ship is sinking." Which leaves us with the yacht.

In the past the term applied to particularly fast vessels. Perhaps yachts nowadays are still fast, but one usually finds them anchored at fashionable resorts where they serve as an exquisite party venue for the prosperous. There are yachts larger than small cruise ships that

are still defined as a yacht to emphasise their luxuri-
ousness. Any self-respecting sheik owns such a sea-
going vessel but prefers travelling to the next port in
his private jet. These decadent, extravagant swimming
palaces are often the object of envy, even among pam-
pered cruisaders.

A cruise ship host once hit on an ingenious idea to
entertain his guests. While the ship was anchored at St.
Tropez he amused the guests to be dropped off at the
little fishing village and residence of Brigitte Bardot in
the following fashion. Equipped with a megaphone,
he shouted over to the yacht dwellers: "Your poverty
disgusts me!" This was greeted by exuberant laughter
not just from the passengers on his tender, but also by
those on several others and thereafter he frequently
indulged his guests with the same performance. Until
he was called to the bridge. The reason: Resident on
his yacht during that fated time was a famous fashion
designer who understood the joker's language as well
as being able to read. He had quickly established the
name of the ship and its company's headquarters and
phoned them. This stopped the joker, but for the sake
of consistency he should have shouted one last time:
"I can only presume you were to mean to send a mes-
senger!"

# ZZZ

Zzzz as in time to lay this guide to rest on your bedside locker and have a little snooze after this, the last chapter. Here goes:

When you arrive back home after a wonderful cruise and you are horrified that your cabin, i.e. your house, hasn't been magically cleaned in your absence, don't make the novice's mistake of hanging the sign "Please clean cabin" you have appropriated as a souvenir (also see Souvenirs) on your front door. It won't work. Three days on at the latest you will notice that nobody picks up the towels that you've so carelessly flung on the floor the way you did for the previous fortnight. This is the point the depression which started on your return journey generally reaches its climax. But it doesn't have to come to that. The experienced cruisader knows that the only way to combat this emotional low is to regale others with his adventures.

The suitcase hasn't even been unpacked and he's still wearing the Bermuda shorts from the last pool party aboard in the Yorkshire Dales in December when the ex-voyager contacts his relatives, phones his friends and meets his neighbours to tell them all about the luxury and other merits a cruise has to offer. He illustrates this with photos and video clips and proudly displays salvaged treasures such as the ship's towels, bathrobes and shower gel (also see Souvenirs). Reactions are mixed. Relatives and other people who still owe him money undividedly share his enthusiasm. Even better, they augment his ramblings with knowledge acquired from watching countless TV reports and swear they'll soon embark on a cruise themselves. A particularly critical individual will now love to ruin the euphoric mood with phrases such as "package tourism". This is where the cruisader's true friends have to prove themselves and rigorously verbally bludgeon the killjoy. And then there are those who after listening to the informative and impassioned voyager's tales claim: "It just not for me. All that time on the water. I don't think it would agree with me." But those are just excuses from those who can't afford a cruise or are simply too stingy.

And here's one last tip: should the final part of the cruise, i.e. impressing your envious neighbours, have appealed to you the most, but you belong to the fringe group who can't afford to pay for a holiday like that or you are too mean to part with your money, the preceding pages may prove to be of help when you want to fabricate your own seafaring tales. A few photo reproductions from holiday brochures and various illustrated volumes, a little skilful Photoshop manipulation and a couple of hours under the sunbed  will suffice to awe the begrudgers and critics with your incredible cruise ship adventures when you've actually spent those ten days in cheap lodgings in Margate.

Have fun and Ship Ahoy!

Don't worry! It's not quite over yet. Here's another alphabetical entry under **H** for

## HIGHLIGHTS

Crew members generally keep a record of the passengers' most ludicrous questions and suggestions. You are already familiar with some of them, but we don't want to deprive you of the rest. In ascending order of scurrility they are -

# PASSENGERS' 10 MOST BIZARRE QUESTIONS:

## 10. Does the crew also sleep on board?

The crew's stock response: We don't. Each night we transfer to a more luxurious cruise ship that is following this one unobtrusively.

## 9. Does this lift go to the front or the back of the ship?

The crew's stock response: Well, a lift primarily goes up or down.

## 8. How do I recognise my photo at the photo shop when my cabin number isn't written on it?

The crew's stock response: Just take a look in the mirror and compare the results.

## 7. Does the crew eat the guests' leftovers from the restau-rant?

The crew's stock response: No, it's the other way around. The place is, after all, called a RESTaurant.

## 6. What do you do with the ice sculptures when they've melted?

The crew's stock response: We wrap them up for you to take home.

## 5. Do non-EU citizens have to take part in the sea rescue drill? (This question was posed by a Swiss gentleman.)

The crew's stock response: Yes, but, of course, Swiss nationals have their own lifeboat; it's a little slower, has numbered accounts on board and serves a tasty fondue.

## 4. How high is the rate of unemployment among the crew?

The crew's stock response: We have close to full employment.

## 3. Did the ship ever sink?

The crew's stock response: Absolutely, and you've no idea how long it took to blow-dry it.

## 2. Does the Captain do this full-time?

The crew's stock response: No, most captains moonlight as cashiers at their local supermarket.

## 1. Is the water in the toilets drinking or saltwater?

The crew's stock response: Why don't you try it? But a warning to those wearing dentures: you are dealing with vacuum toilets, so hold onto your false teeth when flushing.

## Passengers' 5 most absurd suggestions:

**5.** Shore excursions also on days spent at sea

**4.** Drink dispensers on the lifeboats

**3.** Barbecue facilities in the cabin

**2.** On board cable TV

**1.** Inside cabins with balcony

# THE TEST

Cruises are allegedly addictive. The authors have therefore devised a test for you to determine how badly affected you are. After completing the test, simply add the number of **Yes** answers to find out.

You spent more than 184 days per annum on the high seas and are accordingly only subject to limited taxation in your home country. **(Yes / No)**

Your pension is lodged straight into the cruise company's account. **(Yes / No)**

You are on first name terms with most of the officers. **(Yes / No)**

The Captain is your kids' godfather. **(Yes / No)**

You are the shuffleboard champion of the century. **(Yes / No)**

You know the bingo rules off by heart in at least 10 different languages **(Yes / No)**

You are familiar with the personal circumstances of at least 90 % of the crew. **(Yes / No)**

Your passport has no more room for stamps. **(Yes / No)**

In the past 5 years you've visited Cape Horn more often than you've seen your own mother. **(Yes / No)**

The crew consults you should problems arise. **(Yes / No)**

# YOUR SCORE

You ansered **Yes** to all 10 questions: You are hopelessly addicted with no chance of recovery.

You answered **Yes** to 6 or more questions: You are severely addicted, but with intensive therapy you do, however, have a 20% chance of recovery.

You answered **Yes** to 3 or more questions: You are acutely at risk. But if you seek immediate help, you have a good chance of a full recovery.

Get well soon!!!